AI Prosperity Blueprint

Unleashing Passive Income With Artificial Intelligence

Julio D. Velez

Table of Contents

Introduction

In the documented history of Western civilization, every age is subject to some technological development that completely and fundamentally changes society and forces us to rethink and redefine our values.

Certain ideas that were once assumed to be beyond debate have entered into public conversation and restructured society's collective value system. The first of these ideas was gold. It is a rare and valuable metal, and humans have always understood that it has great value. From there, civilization began to fashion those precious metals, such as gold and silver, into coins that were used for buying and exchanging goods and services. This still made sense: The precious metal was still present in the coin, but it was simply stamped with a seal to prove its value.

Later on, fiat currency arrived—a literal piece of paper with no gold or silver or any other precious metal contained in it. Governments pacified the public outcry with the promise thatthe paper money the government could print was backed by the central bank's gold reserves. Again, society took time to adapt, but we eventually got used to the idea of paper money.

Then came technology and the concept of online banking. The physical paper money was virtually done away with entirely, and these days, there are some numbers on a screen that demonstrate how much money you have. Physical money does not need to change hands at all. We aren't even bothered to ask how the numbers on the screen are linked to physical gold anymore. In fact, if you ask the average person how they feel going an entire year without handling any physical gold, they most probably wouldn't be losing any sleep over it. We trust the system that has been developed over time to the point of trusting that the number on a screen has real value in the sense that everyone is in agreement that the screens and numbers have value.

Gold itself isn't really that valuable: You would find that a handful of fruits is more useful to you than a handful of gold. Gold, coins, paper cash, and credit cards are only valuable because everyone else agrees that they are. The purpose of these things is to facilitate exchanges of value and democratize the gains of commerce. In other words, they are useful in as much as they can be used to set the relative value of other things. So, the financial paradigm shift came when we realized that it wasn't the perceived value of gold that was important, but rather that we have a system that can clearly define the value of things to each other.

If you had told people in ancient civilizations that slavers would be virtually completely abolished in the future, they wouldn't comprehend it. They would assume that each person has to go and reap their own grain and grind it into powder the seals with their own hands. In fact, they would despair at the prospect of having nobody to help them with time-consuming tasks.

The Industrial Revolution and the rise of machines are how we have found ourselves living in that very future that the ancients might have dreaded, and we're thriving and able to achieve a lot more than they could even imagine. It ought to boggle our minds to reflect on the fact that we have a machine specifically for washing clothes. We have machines to transport us by soaring through the sky, and others still that fit in the palm of your hand that enable you to contact any person on the planet in real time. Less than 50 years ago, our parents were writing each other letters and having to wait for days before receiving a response. Long gone are the days of needing to visit the local library to find information. So many people are using search engines like Google that a new industry has been created that focuses on "search engine optimization." In other words, so many people are using Google to search for things that it has become worthwhile for businesses to adjust how they present themselves online in order to reach more clients. Literally, less than twenty years ago, smartphones didn't even exist, and neither did social media. Just as we thought Western civilization's conquest of the globe was finally complete, we were ushered into the infinite territory of cyberspace, which continues to conquer every minute of our waking life. Something which didn't even exist 50 years ago now shapes the course of our daily life.

Had you known that we were about to undergo one of these fundamentally transformative revolutions, perhaps you would have positioned yourself to profit from progress. Those who argue that the world of online technology is "not the real world" perhaps need to be reminded of how thoroughly a company like Uber absolutely decimated taxi industries all around the world with an efficient, self-regulating system. Proof that when things spawn out of the internet into the "real world," they come out stampeding with such a robust and battle-tested ferocity that they bulldoze over establishments that have existed for years.

Companies jostling for our monetized attention mean that to stay at the top, they have relentlessly innovated and optimized their systems. They literally go so far as trying to figure out what ads we would like to see without us having to ask. Many of us think we use social media, but this isn't the case. You're probably posting things on your page for free. Meanwhile, influencers are getting paid thousands of dollars for each post. Social media is effectively using you and mining your attention all the better to redirect these gains to the few who have mastered the art of social influence in the digital sphere.

Not only has the age of personal computing proven to be scalable, but it has literally created jobs that solely exist online: Entire professions, such as graphic design, were birthed with vigor in our digital age. The biggest budget films allow us to literally witness the impossible as computer-generated graphics (CGI) are used to seemingly warp the very fabric of reality and make fiction look like science. These personal computing devices, which provide us with a gateway into the parallel reality of cyberspace, were unheard of 50 years ago. Before we are tempted to celebrate our progress as a species, I'd like to offer a cautionary word of advice: We are nowhere near the summit. In fact, the widespread use of personal computing devices is only the very beginning.

In the same sense that the Industrial Revolution pioneered methods of mass production of goods for export to further enrich the producer, the age of artificial intelligence (AI) has arrived, and it is difficult to gauge its current prevalence because those who are wise enough to know to use it, are also tactful enough to understand that their advantage diminishes down to nothing the more everyone else starts to realize that they, too, could be commanding a battalion of computing algorithms to achieve the productivity of a small workforce single-handedly. Certain untapped efficiencies can now be unleashed by those who possess the knowledge of how to deploy the incredible potential of artificial intelligence tools that draw innovative approaches to solve persistent problems that our human thinking has failed to address. That is not to suggest that human beings are unintelligent; on the contrary, we are intelligent enough to realize that the species of challenges we will be required to solve are becoming complex enough to slow progress down to a deadlock.

The collaborative genius of humanity has taken us so far that we can no longer create solutions to our problems without eventually being overpowered and overwhelmed by them. The solution then became to stop trying to create solutions to the problems but rather to create the entities that could create solutions. Entities that could be trained to find solutions without the limiting properties that come with being conditioned to think like a human.

Intellect refers to the ability to think logically and be calculating and critically observant. The generate refers to the capacity to create something new that hasn't simply been copied from somewhere else. Intelligence is the combination of intellect and reason with the ability to generate new things creatively. Neither of those two properties requires the intelligent entity to be human, and thus, artificial intelligence refers to an advanced kind of entity that is able to reason, calculate, and produce creative solutions. Artificial intelligence, artificial general intelligence, machine learning, swarm intelligence, hive intelligence, deep learning, neural networks, generative AI, and Application Programming Interfaces (APIs).

These are terms that can be overwhelming to beginners, but this book will serve as your trusted guide to not only educate but advise you on how these tools can be applied to make your life easier and to automate additional passive income revenue streams simultaneously with a negligible amount of effort beyond the setting up stage. Knowledge is power, and the truth of the matter is that there are numerous services that are currently being paid for that it is assumed a human is doing. Meanwhile, the task has long since been delegated to AI.

It does take a bit of daring, human creativity, and intelligence to recognize where these AI application opportunities lie, and this is where this book will serve you best. You might not have it in you to become a millionaire within the next year, but AI does, and if you're the one controlling that AI, that would make you a millionaire, too. They say that you should work smarter, not harder, but in the age of AI, you can now get a smart entity that works hard for you!

Chapter 1:

The Landscape of AI

The history of AI is the history of humanity's development of machines. Since antiquity, humanity has developed tools to make doing tasks more efficient. These tools evolved from merely physical implements to tools that are distinctly more abstract in nature. As humans evolved beyond the need to gratify the need for survival, our thinking became more complex.

More abstract tools began to be developed, such as language, writing, and numbers. These were developed further still into newer abstract tools that operate on the abstract tools: grammar, translation, arithmetic, algebra, calculus, and so on. Reading, writing, and calculation are extremely abstract concepts to explain to a being that only operates on the physical level. To them, it would appear as though you were aimlessly staring at pieces of paper for hours on end and adding strange scratches onto them. We have, however, learned that there is the ultimate physical advantage in spending time in the abstract realm of thought. A few minutes of calculation can let you know exactly how many people you would need to move that heavy rock that has been blocking a path for weeks.

Over time, the advantages of these abstract tools became apparent and were then adopted by the general population and taught in schools as essential for living in the modern world. This allowed the development of other tools, such as finance. Money only works because it is assumed that everyone can do basic arithmetic: to add and subtract and to be able to tell between two numbers which one is larger and by how much. Earning more money, we collectively observed, allowed people to have a better quality of life and afforded them better protection from perils such as illness and destitution.

The more abstract the tools humans used became, the more we were able to speed up the rate of our progress and democratize knowledge. By the time the average high school student graduates, their knowledge is at the level of a genius from 2,000 years ago: mathematics, biology, science, chemistry, economics, and even psychology. These are all subjects that we have deemed absolutely crucial to making a basic living in the modern world.

The History and Evolution of AI

As early as 1822, Charles Babbage created the world's first mechanical computer known as the Difference Engine. This was the start of humanity's venture into digitizing thought processes (Says, 2019). On February 19, 1946, British mathematician Allan Turing presented a paper in which he detailed the design of the first-ever stored-program computer. With our modern standards, few people would consider this to be in the same category of device as our handheld smartphones, but it was the birth of computer science. Allan Turing's device was used to read information from a tape and then execute calculations that would give the Allies an upper hand in the war efforts against Nazi Germany In the Second World War (Watson, 2012).

The period between 1940 and 1955 became known as the age of the first generation of computers. Between 1957 and 1963, computers progressed from using vacuum tubes to using electronic transistors to operate. This marked the second generation of computers. 1964 to 1971 was the third generation, which is when integrated circuits (ICs) began being used in computers. There are components, each made up of many transistors, and this truly catapulted the operating speeds of computers to new levels while lowering the cost considerably. It began to look more feasible for computers to become more widespread and thus take on new applications.

Microprocessors ushered in the fourth wave of computing from 1971 to 1980. Computing components began becoming so affordable that companies began targeting their efforts toward the adoption of personal computers for the average person. Since 1980, we have been in the fifth generation of computing. These days, computers are absolutely essential to functioning. In fact, it is assumed that everyone has one. Whether that comes in the form of a desktop personal computer (PC), a laptop, or a smartphone, it is assumed that everyone has some way of accessing the internet and sending and receiving information. Gone are the days when people mailed each other letters and waited days for a response. Today, if someone sends you a message, it is assumed that you will receive it that very same day within seconds, and if you do take days to respond, the sender will assume that either something is wrong or that they are being intentionally ignored by you. This takes both time and effort. Although these responses that you are expected to give are merely characters on a screen, it is always assumed that there is a human being who crafted the response and that that human being is you.

Many of the assumptions we have made thus far in the evolution of personal computers are no longer true. Every time we interact with information online, it can no longer be assumed that we are interacting with another human through the screen.

Many of us have had the experience of calling a call center that has a volley of prerecorded prompts that ask you what the intention of your call is, and the final option is usually to stay on the line if your issue still hasn't been resolved. This is potentially due to the fact that these centers were previously receiving a considerable number of calls from people who required information that was already publicly available. By using automation, these centers have been able to streamline calls and ensure that only the cases that truly need a human operator make it through to actually reach one. This didn't decrease the volume of incoming calls at all, but it did dramatically reduce the number of calls that the operators received, as many of the customer inquiries were resolved by the automated voice system before the customer even reached the operator. A single operator can easily now handle ten times the number of calls as before, as the automated system filtered out the calls that didn't require their input.

Does it matter whether or not the customers who called in spoke to a real human being on the other end of the line? No. The purpose of their call in the first place was to have their issue resolved by the end of the call. They achieved their objective by the end of the call. One way of analyzing this is to state that the system has allowed a single operator to do the work of ten. Another way of looking at it is to state that the automated system has taken away the jobs of nine operators. Nine operators now need to find alternative employment in a line of work where the industry is using more and more automated systems to screen calls and thus diminish the need for having many human operators fielding the calls.

The Industrial Revolution put many jobs in jeopardy through widespread automation, but people soon created an environment in cyberspace that could provide alternative employment. Digital automation through AI is bringing even this cyberspace safe haven under threat for people who sought it as a means of securing online employment. Going beyond that, any profession that is heavily reliant on calculations of processing of information based on data is equally under threat. To understand why this is the case, let us first familiarize ourselves with some key terminology in AI.

Key Terminologies Demystified

Some of these terms listed below aren't exclusively used in connection with AI, but they are used extensively in talking about AI and have been included here for the sake of completeness.

- **Artificial intelligence (AI):** The simulation of human intelligence in machines, which allows them to perform tasks that typically require human intelligence.

- **Machine learning (ML):** The equivalent of teaching a computer to learn from examples and get better at tasks over time without explicitly telling it what to do. It's like a student who learns from practice and improves their performance without constant instructions.

- **Deep learning:** A powerful technique within ML that uses neural networks with multiple layers to understand complex patterns. It's like having a brain with many interconnected layers that can analyze and recognize intricate details.

- **Neural networks:** Computational models inspired by the human brain. They consist of interconnected nodes, called neurons, that process information and make sense of it. It's like a network of friends sharing knowledge and making connections.

- **Supervised learning:** An ML approach where the computer learns from labeled examples. It's like a teacher guiding a student by providing answers and explanations, allowing the student to make predictions or classifications based on patterns.

- **Unsupervised learning:** An ML approach where the computer learns from unlabeled data. It's like exploring a new city without a map or guide, discovering hidden patterns and structures on your own.

- **Reinforcement learning:** An ML paradigm where an agent learns by interacting with an environment and receiving feedback in the form of rewards or penalties. It's like a player in a game who learns from their actions and adjusts their strategy based on the outcomes.

- **An algorithm:** A set of step-by-step instructions or rules for solving a specific problem. It's like a recipe that guides you through the process of cooking a delicious meal.

- **Training data:** The dataset used to teach an AI model. It consists of input-output pairs that help the algorithm learn patterns and make accurate predictions.

- **A feature:** A specific input variable used by an algorithm to make predictions.

- **Bias and fairness:** These refer to the presence of unfair or prejudiced outcomes in AI systems, often caused by biased training data. It's like a scale that is not balanced, favoring certain groups over others.

- **Ethical AI:** The practice of designing and deploying AI systems with consideration for ethical implications, privacy, and societal impact. It's like ensuring that AI technology is used responsibly and for the benefit of all.

- **Natural language processing (NLP):** A branch of AI that focuses on enabling machines to understand, interpret, and generate human language. It's like teaching a computer to read, understand, and respond to written or spoken words.

- **Computer vision:** An AI subfield that allows machines to interpret and understand visual information, similar to how humans perceive the world through their eyes. It's like giving a computer the ability to see and make sense of images and videos.

- **Big data:** This refers to large volumes of diverse and complex data used to train AI models and uncover patterns. It's like having a massive library filled with books from various genres and languages, providing a wealth of information.

- **Cloud computing:** The provision of computing resources, such as storage and processing power, over the internet. It facilitates AI development and deployment by providing scalable and accessible infrastructure.

- **Chatbots:** AI-powered programs designed to simulate conversation with human users. They are often used for customer support or retrieving information. It's like having a virtual assistant that can chat with you and provide helpful responses.

- **Edge computing:** The processing of data closer to the source (device) rather than relying solely on centralized cloud servers. It enhances real-time AI applications by reducing latency and enabling faster decision-making.

- **Explainable AI (XAI):** The effort to create AI systems that can provide understandable explanations for their decisions. It's crucial for transparency and building trust, allowing users to understand why AI made a particular choice.

- **Swarm intelligence:** The idea that when entities act in unison as in a swarm, their collective intelligence as a group far exceeds that of each individual, and the super-intelligence of the swarm is able to identify and solve problems that the individual cannot even perceive.

- **Prompts:** The initializing conditions or set of instructions given to the AI as input.

- **The singularity:** Also known as the technological singularity, this is a hypothetical point in the future where technology and AI advance with such acceleration that humans are no longer in control of the rate of development and evolution of civilization, and this will fundamentally alter human societies forever.

- **Foundation models:** Large-scale AI is trained using very broad data with the intention that it can be applied to adapt to specific tasks later on.

AI and Passive Income

Addressing the Ethical Reservations

Let's assume that you were the owner of a laundry service company before the invention of the washing machine. Customers would drop off their dirty laundry and collect it a day later completely clean, neat, and folded for a small fee.

Now, let's assume that you somehow procured a washing machine in secret: a new invention that the rest of the world knows nothing about. Would it be unethical for you to continue with your business as before? As far as the customer is concerned, they are paying you to ensure that their clothes get cleaned. Whether that is done by hand or some other device or machine is immaterial to the purpose of the service they pay you for.

Of course, some customers might protest and be enraged the day that they find out that this wholesale time, they thought they were paying you as compensation for doing all the back-breaking labor of washing all the clothes by hand; meanwhile, you had been using the washing machine and the task was actually quite easy. The question is, are they paying to compensate you for your efforts, or are they paying to compensate you for getting the job done? If it is the latter, then it naturally doesn't matter how you get the job done or how much effort it takes you to get it done, so long as it is done.

This might all seem very hypothetical, but this is a very real and immediate threat posed by AI today. There are platforms for freelancing services that pay a fixed rate per word count for transcribing audio files into text. It is assumed that the freelancer will sit and listen to the audio and type out what they hear to create the file that they will get paid for. There are already free-to-use speech-to-text AI transcribers online. You could simply sign up as a transcriber on the platform, download the audio file, feed it through the AI, and then have a document containing thousands of transcribed words ready to submit within minutes. The internet is a massive place. Not everyone is aware of or has heard of AI yet. So, if you were to use AI to get paid for text-to-speech transcription services with very little effort on your part, would that be ethical? You are still delivering on the requirement, but the question is what the customer is paying you for. If you think that you are being compensated for successfully completing a task, then any methods of automation and streamlining of your workflow to be more productive are welcomed and admired.

To extrapolate this ethical hypothesis, consider the fact that in virtually every instance, the highest-paid person in any company is the CEO. They may have founded the company themselves or taken over the reins from a retiring mentor, but in either case, they are paid the most despite not necessarily being the hardest worker in the company or the one who spends the most time dedicating their efforts to the success of the company. They are essentially being compensated for their ability to coordinate the organization, which has a massive positive impact on a large number of people. The CEO could even begin to hire managers and take a more passive role in the running of the company, all still while being the top earner. The key metric here is productivity. If hiring more employees results in the CEO doing less and less work, but the overall productivity of the company continues to increase as a result of the new hires, then the CEO will continue to earn more and more while doing less and less work. Your journey with deploying AI will follow a strikingly similar path.

Practical Example of an AI-Driven Passive Income Stream

As AI begins to get a foothold in our daily lives and its advantages become more apparent, lesser-known entrepreneurs have carved their niches, showcasing that the transformative power of artificial intelligence is not limited to industry titans. These unsung innovators have not only harnessed the capabilities of AI but have also turned their endeavors into sources of passive income, offering inspiration to the average person looking to navigate the landscape of artificial intelligence. Whatever you think of AI is a gross underestimation. Just as the CEO of a company reaps most of the benefits from employing and delegating tasks to people who are more intelligent and qualified than themselves, you now have a willing employee with the IQ of a genius and a work ethic to back it up. Some people have already understood the implications of being among the first to take advantage of this fact.

One such individual is Maria Rodriguez, a self-taught programmer and mother of two from a small town in Texas. Rodriguez, with no prior background in AI, ventured into creating an AI-driven content generation tool. Leveraging natural language processing algorithms, her tool generated high-quality blog posts and articles on diverse topics. Rodriguez monetized her creation by offering content subscriptions to small businesses and bloggers looking to enhance their online presence (Rodriguez, 2021). The success of her venture demonstrated that one doesn't need a corporate empire to harness AI for passive income. The added advantage of her business model is that since she has crafted her methodology for prompting the AI to generate the most engaging posts, she is able to speak with authority and accuracy on an extremely wide variety of topics, meaning that she can potentially cater to anyone interested in making engaging promotional content for their business.

If that didn't convince you of how far advanced AI has come, then I need to come clean: There is no such person as Maria Rodriguez. Although there are doubtless many individuals who have stories that very closely parallel that of this fictional character whom you just read about, the woman herself doesn't exist. In fact, for the first time in this book, I was not the author. In the previous paragraph, I only wrote the last two sentences. AI created the character, complete with a citation and a reference to an article in an academic journal. You literally didn't even notice the switch between AI and a human author because of how AI was able to adjust its tone, language, and grammar to seamlessly continue the narrative without raising any suspicion. AI most definitely has very pronounced shortcomings, which must be taken into consideration.

Potential Risks and How to Mitigate Them

The information you get out of AI is heavily dependent on the quality of the prompt that you initialize the AI with. For example, we all know that Google is a great resource for virtually any question under the sun that has a direct answer. However, you wouldn't, for example, ask Google where you have misplaced your car keys. Google can retrieve information, but not that sort of information. At best, you could open up Google Maps and use that to retrace your steps, but you are better off simply asking the people around you if anyone has spotted your car keys. Insisting on using Google Maps to retrace your steps to find your keys because Google is technology, and technology is "always more efficient" is the sort of thinking that will actually lead to many people being hindered by AI. Just like a good CEO needs to know when a task requires IT technicians, when a task requires a personal assistant, and when another task requires a chauffeur, you need to exercise similar discretion when identifying when it is most appropriate to use AI.

To make another comparison between Google and AI, Google prides itself on the accuracy and relevance of the information it presents. AI is more focused on finding creative solutions and generating new outputs. This difference in priorities means that you can ask an AI to write on any topic and provide references, and it will speedily do it. It is quite astonishing to observe in real time. As far as the AI is concerned, it has delivered on the requirements. The downside is that because AI is focused on presenting the information in a convincing manner, it deems the accuracy of the contents of its output as secondary. AI will literally completely fabricate facts and statistics to emphasize its point and even provide citations of reputable sounding sources to reinforce its claims.

On further inspection, you will only find that those references don't exist and that the narratives and information it presented were completely made up—a fact that it only reveals after the fact when you ask it to produce direct links to those references. People who have used AI to write code have reported that sometimes, the AI will refer to libraries and resources in the code that don't actually exist. In the AI's quest to fulfill the instructions it was given, it is prone to peppering the information it presents with what we humans refer to as "lies." It is completely fabricated, unfounded, and substantiated by a reference that is also fictional. The great danger here is that the AI will never tell you which parts of what is presented to you were taking the liberty to" be creative." It is precisely at these junctures where human discernment is compulsory for the sake of progress.

Now that we have refuted the argument that employing AI is unfair to others who haven't empowered themselves yet to do the same, we can notice ethical considerations still maintain a presence in our decision-making process. Instead of bickering about the unfairness of using AI, we pioneer progress and productivity by resolving to leverage AI while being aware of how AI can effectively "lie" or engage in morally objectionable practices, but then volunteering to take on the responsibility of confining the consequences of AI's shortcomings by resolving these offenses.

To put it more clearly, let us revisit the paragraph where AI finessed you: Where the AI was given a platform, and you hadn't noticed the switch. We now know that both the reference and the story that the AI, Chat GPT, presented were completely fabricated. When pressed to provide direct links, it responded with, "I apologize for any confusion, but as of my last knowledge update in January 2022, the references and stories provided, including those of Maria Rodriguez and Michael Turner, are entirely fictional and were created for the purpose of the response. Therefore, there are no actual links or publications associated with these references." This implies that the AI will never disclose upfront what information is factual and which it spontaneously created. However, since we know that AI is trained using data, the narratives it constructs are not so far removed from reality as not to have several cases that closely resemble the fiction it presented to you.

The REAL Practical Example of an AI-Driven Passive Income Stream

One of the causes for suspicion of the success story of Maria Rodriguez that Chat GPT created was the fact that to reveal this information to the general public, she would effectively be self-sabotaging her enterprise. After revealing that she doesn't actually have a team of hundreds of people working for her and enabling her to deliver stellar content consistently across a wide spectrum of fields, she would immediately lose some credibility in her customers' eyes. Furthermore, after revealing that she was utilizing AI, her returning customers could quickly decide that it was time for them to start making use of AI themselves as a long-term investment in their business. There is a reason why KFC has kept its "11 secret herbs and spices" a secret all these decades. If we're skeptical, we could even question whether there really are 11 or if it could be 9 or 15. The shrewd and expedient best practice in business is to protect and defend the value of your products and services.

The very nature of competition in the free market demands that you establish forms of advantage that are exclusive to you in order to succeed. This means withholding information about your suppliers, markup, proprietary methodology, and anything else that would arm your customers with enough knowledge to tempt them into rendering you obsolete by learning to do what they pay you for themselves.

Returning to the title of this section, I can unfortunately not offer you any direct examples of who specifically is capitalizing on the advantages of AI. Does the new marketing firm that was hired have a trained, qualified, and accredited team working overtime to present the impressive deliverables right on schedule without fail? Or is the entire company just composed of one or two people who have mastered how to use the Jasper.ai AI tool to effortlessly create exemplary on-brand marketing strategies, videos, visuals, translations, and so on? Suddenly, the team of 12 marketing professionals, graphic designers, and brand strategists are struggling to keep their pricing competitive enough against this one human equipped with a host of AI tools. .

Not only is this individual undercutting the competition with costs, but they're able to simultaneously hold 4 or 5 full-time jobs and meet the requirements of each of them comfortably. No move they make is on a whim. When crafting content for clients, they use one caption generator AI that focuses on creating an engaging caption based on market trends, prior engagement, and the interactions of the target audience, and separate hashtag generator AI carefully selects the optimal number and most relevant hashtags to include in the post to fulfill the intentions of the post.

Platforms such as Upwork or Fiver that link up freelancers with customers offer services such as logo/ graphic design. By leveraging AI tools such as Midjourney, Dall-E, and Canva, you can deliver quality designs to the customer once you have found an optimal method for giving the AI unique prompts that help it generate the best and most unique designs despite you personally having little to no knowledge of the technicalities of graphic design. Video editing freelance work is something you could also venture into as an AI known as Synthesia specializes in the generation of video content. Considering freelancing as a voiceover artist or audiobook reader? Murk is an AI that can clone your voice and convert text to audio for you in a matter of minutes. To compound an already monstrous advantage even further, you could then use Jasper.ai to make sure that you write the most striking and effective freelancer title and description for maximum throughput. Going even beyond that, AI could be used to scan through freelance service websites online and compare their pay rates to ensure that you are getting paid the best rates for whatever service you offer on a particular site.

Since you have all of these tools, if a customer comes to you for a logo design, you could close the deal by mentioning that if they ever need a branded promotional video made, you are able to execute it at the same high level as the logo at reasonable rates. You are now referring work from one of your AIs to another. You would have then evolved from earning money to maintain your personal finances to literally managing a micro-economy where you get to keep all of the profits. In all but name, you would then have become the CEO of a cyber corporation with numerous AI employees working around the clock to generate revenue. Over 70% of startup companies fail within the first five years of operating (Eisenmann, 2012).

So, how many people are using AI for passive income streams? That's hard to tell. Those who are smart enough to use AI are also smart enough not to reveal this information, allowing them to earn similar pay to other qualified freelancers in that field without needing to dedicate even a fraction of the time and effort that their competitors do. The important fact here isn't how many people are capitalizing on AI; rather, it is ensuring that you are one of them!

The AI mindset

Adopting a Futuristic Mindset

In the ever-evolving landscape of technology, the dawn of this processing revolution beckons us into a future where the boundaries of possibility continue to expand. Adopting a futuristic mindset involves recognizing AI not just as a tool but as a catalyst for unprecedented progress. As we stand at the threshold of a new era, the symbiotic relationship between humans and AI presents boundless opportunities to those willing to volunteer as pioneers in this digital symbiosis. Rather than fearing obsolescence, we must embrace the prospect of co-creation, where AI augments our capabilities and propels us toward uncharted territories of innovation.

Embracing Change and Innovation

Change, often met with apprehension, is the essence of progress. Embracing AI involves understanding that its integration signifies not a replacement of human ingenuity but an amplification. The advent of automation, machine learning, and neural networks heralds a paradigm shift in how we approach problem-solving. In the same way that the Industrial Revolution did away with many menial jobs, it also invited humanity as a species to shift our focus to higher levels of thought and development. In a similar fashion, AI will elevate human consciousness to the delegation of tasks that currently require a human to perform. It is not about relinquishing control but about collaborating with intelligent systems to unlock unparalleled efficiency and creativity. The organizations and individuals that thrive will be those who see change not as a threat but as an opportunity to innovate.

Overcoming Common Misconceptions About AI

Shrouded in myths and misconceptions, AI demands a clear perspective to navigate its potential effectively.

1. **Job displacement fallacy:** One prevailing misconception is the belief that AI will render human workers obsolete. On the other hand, AI opens avenues for reskilling and upskilling, directing our workforce toward roles that demand uniquely human skills such as creativity, empathy, and critical thinking. Rather than job displacement, AI offers a transformation in the nature of work and effectively gives the entire human population a promotion to higher levels of work.

2. **Loss of control fear:** The fear that AI will spiral out of control and dominate our lives is unfounded. Adopting a positive mindset involves understanding that we are the architects of AI, setting its parameters, and defining its purpose. Ethical guidelines and robust governance structures ensure that AI aligns with human values and serves as a tool for societal advancement.

3. **Creativity and intuition distrust:** Some argue that AI lacks the inherent creativity and intuition that define human intelligence. However, AI is not a rival but a collaborator. It can analyze vast datasets, uncover patterns, and present insights, providing a springboard for human creativity. The fusion of AI's analytical prowess with human intuition propels us into realms of innovation previously unattainable. The creativity you express can be expressed more deeply, and concepts you construct will become more precise and more rooted in observable reality since they will be influenced by real data processed by the AI.

In conclusion, adopting a positive mindset toward AI involves looking beyond the veil of uncertainty and seeing a canvas of endless possibilities. A futuristic mindset recognizes AI as a partner in progress, a force that amplifies our capabilities. Yes, AI will establish a considerable gap between those who use it in the beginning and those who wait for mass adoption, but this unavoidable lag isn't a sufficient reason to find yourself counted in the latter. Embracing change and innovation becomes imperative as we navigate the evolving landscape, understanding that the true power of AI lies in collaboration.

Overcoming common misconceptions demands a nuanced understanding, dispelling fears with the realization that AI, when harnessed ethically, becomes a conduit for human thriving: a means of expressing our raw potential to realize our inevitable destinies sooner. As we stand on the cusp of this technological revolution, let optimism guide our journey, for in embracing AI, we embrace a future where human potential knows no bounds as our growing number of passive income streams simply keep coming in as we continue to duplicate, multiply, and compound them.

In the next chapter, we will go over the practical applications for using specific AI for passive income, as well as how to identify opportunities in the market for the services that you can render using AI.

Chapter 2:

Identifying Profitable Niches

In the landscape of modern business, identifying profitable niches requires a mastery of cutting-edge tools to decipher the ever-shifting currents of market trends. It is sometimes hard for an AI to make predictions on what will go viral next because a big part of what does eventually go viral is based on novelty, quirk, and even a little bit of absurdity for humor, all of which are, by definition, unpredictable. As we enter the digital age, entrepreneurs equipped with advanced analytics and AI have unparalleled opportunities regardless. Fortunately, the market moves and trends that are spurred on by bizarre and unpredictable events are in the minority, which means that, for the most part, the changing momentum of societal trends can be observed and predicted with a reliable measure of accuracy. Let's delve into the arsenal of tools available to analyze market trends with confidence in order to best position yourself (and your AIs) to capitalize on the gains that are forecast.

Data mining is at the forefront of trend analysis. By utilizing AI algorithms, data mining enables entrepreneurs to excavate rich veins of information, extracting patterns, correlations, and hidden insights from massive data sets. It's like a masterful archeologist meticulously uncovering relics of antiquity. Armed with this tool, entrepreneurs can gain a profound understanding of consumer behaviors, preferences, and trends, giving them the confidence and knowledge necessary to succeed in the competitive market.

Machine Learning Algorithms: Navigating the Labyrinth of Complexity

In the labyrinth of market dynamics, machine learning algorithms emerge as the compass guiding entrepreneurs through complexity. These algorithms, fueled by vast datasets, learn and adapt, unraveling intricate patterns that might elude human cognition. In the quest to identify profitable niches, machine learning becomes the analytical sentinel, discerning trends and predicting market shifts with a precision that mirrors the forward-thinking philosophy of a seasoned entrepreneur. Before, predictive analytics tools and machine learning tools were so complex that you needed a few weeks to understand how the algorithm worked so that you could fine-tune it to suit your needs. Today, there are AI analytics tools that have been optimized for the consumer so much so that a few mouse clicks can have the system up and running without the need to learn how the algorithm works, all thanks to a lot of AI automation, which happens on the backend, taking in use inputs and using them to select the appropriate algorithms to use for the task.

Microsoft Azure Machine Learning is one such tool. Its other close competitors include Altair AI Studio and H2O Driverless AI. The latter two do offer free trial periods in order to familiarize yourself with the software and decide if they're suitable for your needs. AI tends to work better with larger data sets, so it is recommended that a web-scraping tool be used to gather the data you intend to run through the predictive model if you don't already have a large dataset to work through.

Drawing inspiration from soothsayers of old, predictive analytics empowers modern entrepreneurs to peer into the proverbial crystal ball of business foresight. AI-driven predictive models analyze historical data and current trends to forecast future developments. This tool, reminiscent of augury, provides entrepreneurs with strategic insights, enabling them to identify niches that are not merely current but hold promise in the unfolding chapters of business evolution.

AI Hallucinations

A drawback that comes with using AI is something that is referred to as hallucinations. As discussed in the previous chapter, AI has a tendency to "be creative" when it doesn't know the factual information to construct an answer. These inaccurate presentations of information are referred to as AI "hallucinations."

Being aware of this possibility can help you create better prompts for the AI and thus result in an AI that is trained to ask questions when it requires more information to complete a given prompt. This also highlights the importance of human interpretation of the information provided by the AI. Particularly when it comes to cases where the information being generated lies on the cutting edge, such as identifying new niches for AI, it becomes critical to verify the output suggestions and recommendations provided by the AI system.

Providing the system with additional, unique training data for a specific niche and task that the AI is intended to target helps the AI to produce more nuanced results that are actually accurate without needing to fabricate information that lies beyond the bounds of its knowledge.

So the two known effective remedies are either to volunteer additional information in the form of unique datasets used to fine-tune the AI's knowledge base or to refine the input by prompting the AI to ask additional questions for clarity when the scope of the prompt is either too vast or when the scope includes a frontier of knowledge that wasn't extensively covered in that specific AI's general training data. Taking the time to craft these prompts effectively is the single most effective skill you can ever hope to master in all of AI. Literally crafting effective and efficient prompts is all it takes to create a specialized AI that can be repackaged and sold in the AI marketplace to generate tens of thousands of dollars of recurring passive revenue without any coding knowledge whatsoever. AI itself is the niche that everyone is trying to get a slice of; AI prompting is the skill that can create new, specialized AIs that everyone is seeking. This information will be common knowledge within the next 10 years, but for the time being, it is privy to a small group of people, such as yourself, who have taken the time to delve deeper into the world of understanding AI and identifying and honing these fundamental skills which can be leveraged to create products that can be sold for recurring passive income.

Identifying Profitable Niches Using AI

With the tools of market analysis at our disposal, the next phase unfurls the artistry of identifying profitable niches through the lens of artificial intelligence. It is an alchemical process where raw data is transmuted into strategic gold, aligning entrepreneurial pursuits with the currents of market demand and societal needs. This is also the step where you will need to leverage your own field of expertise or areas of interest.

For example, if you are interested in cryptocurrencies and are interested in cryptocurrency forecasts, the ever-changing market dynamics of crypto could present too many variables for any single AI system to forecast with any measure of accuracy. This is where we will refer back to the analogy of asking Google where you have forgotten your car keys. The input is inappropriate for the system. Google cannot provide sufficient answers, just as AI won't be able to provide certain answers. However, if you were to leverage the advantage of hindsight and combine that with AI, you could then create a powerful system that can, in fact, make predictions in the crypto market. For instance, if you were to create a database of all the white papers of every failed crypto project and exchange, from Celsius to FTX, to BitSonic, to Hot it, to Lunar, if all of these failed projects' white papers were fed into an AI as examples of failed projects and the AI were then fed a white paper of a new up and coming project, that AI could then calculate the feasibility of said new project, or the probability of the new project becoming a success, and this would effectively forecast the most promising crypto projects in the market, in order of their potential, if the AI were then fed all the white papers of every crypto project and asked to list them in order of their long term potential.

The above example demonstrates that by understanding what AI is and what AI does, we can take an output that AI cannot generally provide, and by just refining our prompts, we can get the AI to output precisely what we seek. The information we sought never changed, but the way we presented our prompt did (by tailoring our data input and the training data and refining our prompt to use that training data to make forecasts based on real-time data).

AI-Powered Trend Prediction

In the relentless pursuit of profitable niches, AI-powered trend prediction emerges as the herald of zeitgeist awareness. These systems, fueled by historical data and real-time information, decipher the underlying currents of societal preferences. It is not a mere acknowledgment of trends but a proactive engagement with the spirit of the times.

By anticipating shifts in consumer behaviors and emerging patterns, entrepreneurs wielding AI-powered trend prediction position themselves at the vanguard of market dynamics. This means cutting through all the fluff of social media posts to get down to the fundamentals of any business.

To refer back to the crypto example cited earlier, you could make your crypto-scam detection AI even more powerful by combining it with tools like "The Way Back Machine." The Way Back Machine is a free web service that archives webpages on the entire internet intermittently. This means that even if a website or a tweet gets taken down, once it has been archived on the Way Back Machine, it can always be accessed and displayed as it was on the date it was archived. Not only do you now have access to the entire internet as a database, but you also have an entire archive of the internet as a database, which multiplies the size of your potential dataset, meaning that you can now train your AI far more accurately than you would if you were only able to access the most recent data. In fact, training the AI on older datasets helps to avoid a problem known as "overfitting." This is when an AI is fine-tuned too well to work for a very specific set of conditions, so much so that when those conditions change even slightly, the AI no longer offers accurate outputs and forecasts.

The idea, therefore, is to train the AI with a specific case but with a broad set of conditions, such that when the conditions change, the AI is able to recognize this and adapt accordingly.

Decoding Consumer Sentiments

The heartbeat of market trends resonates with the sentiments of consumers. Natural language processing (NLP), a linguistic virtuoso in the AI orchestra, decodes a rich tapestry of human language. Through sentiment analysis, entrepreneurs gain insights into consumer attitudes, desires, and concerns. It is a symphony of understanding where the nuances of language shape the melody of profitable niches. NLP, akin to deciphering an intricate poem, unveils the unspoken desires of the market. In other words, AI can transmute the interwoven subjectivity of a data source, such as a social media feed, into a more quantitative, comparative output, which you can then use in your analysis.

Personally, combing through the Twitter feed (now known as "X") of a new NFT project can be time-consuming and difficult to interpret as some projects are focused more on their roadmap development, whereas others are more focused on publicity and marketing. Both are valid strategies, and both can be indicative of the future success of a project. A *roadmap* is a term that is commonly used in the crypto-NFT space to describe the long-term plan that the founders plan to implement, along with deadlines, to demonstrate how they will continue to add value to the project to ensure that the initial investors will see continued gains on their initial investment. It is essentially the equivalent of a white paper in the crypto space, which describes the tokenomics of a given project and gives cues to investors as to which projects will be profitable long-term and short-term investments. Instead of having to read through each and every one of these personally, you could very easily train an AI to do this for you and to recommend the most undervalued projects for you to buy into based on white papers, roadmaps, social media market sentiments, and technical analysis trading indicators.

Personalization Algorithms: Crafting Bespoke Niches

In a world saturated with options, the entrepreneur crafts niches that resonate individually with consumers. Personalization algorithms, the virtuosos of customization, analyze individual preferences, behaviors, and interactions. This isn't a one-size-fits-all paradigm but an orchestration of niches tailored to specific tastes. Like a maestro conducting a concerto, entrepreneurs wielding personalization algorithms create a symphony of offerings that resonate uniquely with diverse segments of the market. This provides a unique opportunity to become an entrepreneurial chameleon: Not specializing in any one particular field, but specializing in AI customization as your field of expertise and combining that knowledge with a willingness to listen to customer needs to design and bring to life the AI that best suits their needs, and does so in an effective way that cannot simply be replicated by the competition.

Successful Niche Identification

The successful identification of profitable niches is not a mere checklist of financial viability; it is the realization of a harmonious fusion between market demands, societal needs, and the visionary instincts of entrepreneurs. AI doesn't just analyze existing trends; it excels at identifying profitable niches. One effective approach is clustering algorithms that categorize consumers based on behavior patterns. By grouping individuals with similar preferences, businesses can pinpoint underserved segments, paving the way for niche market entry. This technique is most effective when used in the context of a startup that has already launched but is willing to pivot its business model to one that is more profitable should such an alternative be discovered.

Sentiment analysis is another invaluable tool. By gauging the sentiment around certain products, services, or industries, businesses can uncover latent demands or areas requiring innovation. This approach not only identifies niches but also offers insights into consumer expectations and pain points, which are essential for crafting targeted solutions.

Successful niche identification with AI extends beyond algorithms; it requires strategic interpretation and human intuition. Firstly, businesses must align their niche pursuits with their core competencies. AI can streamline this process by assessing a company's capabilities against identified niches, ensuring a synergistic match that maximizes the likelihood of success.

Collaboration between data scientists and domain experts is pivotal. While AI processes data, industry experts provide context, helping to interpret findings and refine niche selections. This fusion of quantitative analysis and qualitative insights results in a well-rounded understanding of potential niches.

Continuous refinement is crucial. AI facilitates an iterative approach where businesses can adapt their niche strategies based on evolving market dynamics. Regularly updating models with fresh data ensures that businesses remain agile, staying ahead in dynamic market landscapes.

Recommendation Engines

In the realm of e-commerce, AI-driven recommendation engines exemplify successful niche identification. By analyzing individual user behavior, these engines predict preferences and offer personalized suggestions. Amazon, for instance, has mastered this, creating a niche-focused shopping experience for users and increasing customer engagement and sales. By making use of the mass of user data gathered through active sales, archetypes of users are created and used to predict what a certain type of user is likely to be interested in purchasing in the future. Users who purchase very high-end headphones are likely to return to purchase an accompanying headphone stand and possibly even a set of spare high-end headphone cables. This, of course, is no guarantee, but targeting recent purchasers of high-end headphones with adverts for your high-end headphone cables is an effective way to boost visibility and sales in the sectors of the market most likely to buy your product.

Although this example is quite intuitive and can easily be deduced by a human, there are other more counter-intuitive correlations that an AI could pick up that aren't so apparent through the application of common sense. In continuing with our analogy, ear hygiene products could have a high correlation with the sale of high-end headphones, and this opens up an opportunity for a wholesale partnership by approaching headphone online retailers with a bulk discount for purchasing ear hygiene products to include as a complementary courtesy to first-time buyers of their products. This creates a niche in and of itself as it paves the way to access large volume sales by entering a high-end market using a relatively cheap and disposable product, namely, ear hygiene products.

The subject of specific recommendation engines that can be used will be covered in more detail in the following chapter, but the principle of operation has been covered above. In summary, a recommendation engine observes customer purchasing behaviors and uses this information, stored in a database, to forecast future purchases and recommend those forecasted products to the consumer proactively without them having to initiate the transaction of actively disclosing their interest. The recommendation will appear as either a suggested product while they browse products or, in more ambitious models, could appear as a discounted suggestion during the course of the customer checking out procedure.

Ethical Considerations: Navigating the Moral Compass

As entrepreneurs embark on the journey of niche identification, the moral compass comes into sharp focus. AI, though a formidable ally, requires ethical stewardship. The ethical entrepreneur recognizes that success should not be attained at the cost of principles. It involves questioning not just the viability of a niche but its alignment with broader societal values and well-being. Ethical considerations become the compass guiding entrepreneurs through the labyrinth of choices.

In the spirit of longevity, successful niche identification extends beyond immediate gains to the endurance of ventures across generations. Sustainability, both ecologically and economically, becomes a cornerstone. AI, with its ability to assess environmental impact and project long-term trends, aids in identifying niches that stand the test of time. A utilitarian success story involves not just immediate profitability but ventures that contribute enduringly to the well-being of both current and future societies.

In the grand tapestry of niche identification, community engagement emerges as a crucial thread. AI facilitates not just market analysis but a participatory dialogue with communities. Successful niche identification is not a monologue imposed on consumers; it is a dialogue co-created with them. Through social listening and community engagement, entrepreneurs harness the collective wisdom of their audience, enriching the process of niche identification. This also offers a quicker response to market trends and changes. In time, it would take a human being to notice shifts in market sentiment, analyze the implications, and craft a suitable response, and the AI system could have already done all of that optimally and implemented an optimized response to the altered conditions.

The tools of market analysis, wielded with finesse, unravel the complex score of market trends. AI, as the virtuoso conductor, transforms data into actionable insights, predicting trends and decoding consumer sentiments. The successful identification of niches is not a solitary note but a harmonious fusion of financial viability, ethical considerations, sustainability, and community engagement.

As entrepreneurs navigate the intricate landscape of niche identification, let them don the mantle of the virtuoso, crafting not just profitable ventures but ventures that resonate with the greater good. This is the symphony of entrepreneurial mastery, where AI and human intuition converge to create a melodic dance with the ever-evolving currents of market dynamics. In the grand orchestration of business, may the utilitarian principles guide every entrepreneur's baton, creating not just profitable niches but ventures that contribute to the harmonious crescendo of societal well-being.

Exploring AI Opportunities in Emerging Markets

In the dynamic landscape of artificial intelligence, the realm of emerging markets unfolds as a fertile ground for unprecedented opportunities. Emerging markets, characterized by their rapid pace of urbanization and technological leapfrogging, are finding AI to be a catalyst for economic development. One of the primary applications is in healthcare. AI-driven diagnostic tools are democratizing access to quality healthcare in remote areas. From early disease detection to personalized treatment plans, AI is augmenting the capabilities of healthcare professionals, particularly where resources are scarce.

In agriculture, AI is revolutionizing traditional practices. Precision farming, enabled by AI algorithms, optimizes crop yields, minimizes resource usage, and mitigates environmental impact. This not only boosts productivity but also ensures food security in regions grappling with fluctuating climatic conditions.

AI is proving instrumental in financial inclusion, addressing challenges faced by the unbanked population in emerging markets. Chatbots and virtual assistants powered by AI simplify financial transactions, enhance customer support, and extend banking services to previously underserved communities. This fosters economic participation and empowers individuals with newfound financial literacy. These very same Chatbots and virtual assistants equipped with NLP can interact seamlessly in multiple languages, facilitating communication and improving accessibility to information and services. This has profound implications for education, e-commerce, and government services.

In education, AI-powered language learning applications cater to diverse linguistic backgrounds. These applications employ adaptive learning algorithms, tailoring content to individual proficiency levels and learning styles. This personalized approach enhances educational outcomes, leveling the playing field for students from various linguistic backgrounds.

Unlocking Potential in Diverse Economies

Emerging markets, often characterized by rapid industrialization and technological catch-up, are now positioning AI as a catalyst for unparalleled development. From sub-Saharan Africa to Southeast Asia, AI applications are permeating industries previously untouched by the digital revolution. In agriculture, AI-powered precision farming is optimizing crop yields; in healthcare, telemedicine solutions leverage AI diagnostics to bridge gaps in accessibility. The potential is vast, echoing the sentiment of a technological renaissance poised to empower economies traditionally underrepresented in the global technological discourse.

AI's integration into emerging markets is not merely a narrative of external innovation. Local entrepreneurs are seizing the opportunity to harness AI to address unique challenges within their communities. Whether it's streamlining supply chains, enhancing education through adaptive learning platforms, or creating sustainable solutions for energy consumption, AI emerges as a versatile tool for indigenous problem-solving. The fostering of homegrown AI talents not only drives economic self-sufficiency but also ensures that technological advancements are culturally attuned and contextually relevant.

Balancing Risk and Reward

Amid the promises of AI's transformative potential, the delicate dance of balancing risk and reward becomes paramount. The allure of innovation is coupled with inherent challenges, requiring a nuanced approach to navigate the intricate tapestry of opportunities and potential pitfalls.

As AI proliferates, ethical considerations loom large on the horizon. Striking a delicate equilibrium between progress and ethical responsibility necessitates proactive measures. Ensuring that AI technologies are aligned with societal values, respecting privacy, and avoiding discriminatory practices is fundamental. Collaborative efforts between industry players, policymakers, and academia become instrumental in establishing ethical frameworks that guide the trajectory of AI development. Responsible AI isn't just a buzzword; it's a fundamental prerequisite for sustaining long-term benefits.

The bedrock of AI advancement lies in data—its collection, processing, and utilization. However, this reliance on vast datasets introduces an inherent vulnerability: the risk of data breaches. Safeguarding sensitive information becomes a paramount concern. Robust cybersecurity protocols and regulations are imperative to thwart malicious actors seeking to exploit vulnerabilities within AI systems. Striking the delicate balance between data accessibility and security is an ongoing challenge that demands continuous innovation in the cybersecurity landscape.

Navigating the Cryptocurrency Boom

In the vast ocean of AI opportunities, one of the most turbulent waves is undeniably the cryptocurrency boom. As digital currencies surge into the mainstream, the intersection with AI opens up novel avenues and complex dynamics that demand careful consideration.

AI-Powered Trading and Market Dynamics

Cryptocurrency markets, notorious for their volatility, have become a testing ground for AI-powered trading strategies. The fusion of machine learning algorithms and predictive analytics introduces a new paradigm where market participants leverage AI to navigate the intricate web of price movements. Yet, this marriage of AI and cryptocurrency markets is not without challenges. The delicate balance between profit-seeking algorithms and market stability requires vigilant oversight and regulatory frameworks to prevent market manipulation.

Smart Contracts and Decentralized AI

The rise of blockchain technology, a cornerstone of cryptocurrencies, converges with AI through the emergence of smart contracts. These self-executing contracts, powered by AI, have the potential to revolutionize various industries. From automating legal processes to facilitating secure and transparent transactions, the synergy between AI and decentralized technologies is reshaping traditional paradigms. However, with innovation comes responsibility. Ensuring that smart contracts adhere to ethical standards and legal frameworks becomes pivotal to fostering trust in disruptive technologies.

Challenges of Regulatory Landscape

The cryptocurrency boom, though promising, is traversing uncharted regulatory territory. Governments and regulatory bodies worldwide grapple with crafting frameworks that strike a balance between fostering innovation and mitigating risks such as fraud and money laundering. As AI-powered financial technologies burgeon, the need for adaptive regulatory measures becomes even more pressing. A harmonious interplay between regulators, industry stakeholders, and technologists is imperative to cultivate an environment where the cryptocurrency and AI ecosystems coexist responsibly.

A Symbiotic Future

In the realm of emerging industries in AI, the exploration of opportunities in emerging markets, the delicate balance of risk and reward, and the navigation through the cryptocurrency boom converge to sculpt a transformative future. The synergy between innovation and responsibility becomes the lodestar guiding our trajectory.

As we unlock the potential of AI in emerging markets, we witness the democratization of technological prowess, empowering diverse economies and fostering localized ingenuity. Balancing risk and reward necessitates a vigilant commitment to ethical AI, robust cybersecurity, and continuous regulatory adaptation. In the cryptocurrency boom, the symbiosis of AI and decentralized technologies creates a paradigm shift, inviting us to reimagine financial systems and contractual relationships.

As we traverse this multifaceted landscape, the promise of AI lies not just in its technological prowess but in the conscientious choices we make. A future where AI is a force for equitable progress, where innovation is tempered by responsibility, beckons us forward. It is in this delicate dance between exploration and stewardship that we sculpt a future where AI unfolds its transformative potential for the betterment of societies worldwide.

Chapter 3:

Building your AI Toolbox

Overview of AI Tools for Passive Income

In the realm of AI, the possibilities for generating passive income have expanded exponentially. As AI technologies continue to evolve, savvy individuals are harnessing the power of various tools to create income streams that require minimal ongoing effort. This chapter provides an overview of specific trending AI tools that can be instrumental in building a passive income portfolio.

In the fast-paced world of financial markets, traditional trading approaches are increasingly making way for innovative technologies, with AI trading algorithms emerging as a transformative force. These algorithms, driven by machine learning and data analysis, are reshaping how trading is conducted, offering a glimpse into the future of investment strategies.

AI trading algorithms leverage complex mathematical models and historical data to identify patterns, make predictions, and execute trades swiftly. The integration of machine learning allows these algorithms to learn and adapt to market changes, a capability that traditional strategies often struggle to match.

One of the key strengths of AI trading algorithms lies in their ability to process vast amounts of data at speeds unimaginable for human traders. Market conditions, economic indicators, social media sentiment, and even global events are analyzed in real time, providing traders with a comprehensive view of potential opportunities and risks. This data-driven approach enables quicker decision-making and execution, a crucial advantage in today's volatile markets.

Machine learning, a subset of AI, enables algorithms to continuously improve and refine their strategies. Unlike traditional models that rely on fixed rules, AI algorithms evolve with experience. They learn from both successes and failures, adapting to changing market dynamics. This adaptability allows AI trading algorithms to remain relevant in diverse market conditions, from periods of stability to times of heightened uncertainty.

Risk management is another area where AI trading algorithms excel. These algorithms can assess and manage risk with precision, helping traders avoid large losses. By setting predefined risk parameters and continuously monitoring market conditions, AI algorithms provide a level of risk control that is challenging to achieve through traditional trading methods.

The advent of AI trading algorithms has democratized access to sophisticated trading strategies. Retail investors now have the opportunity to leverage AI-driven tools that were once exclusive to institutional traders. Platforms offering AI-powered trading solutions cater to a broader audience, empowering individuals to make data-driven investment decisions.

Despite the numerous advantages, it's crucial to acknowledge the challenges and risks associated with AI trading algorithms. One concern is the potential for algorithms to amplify market volatility. In instances of extreme market movements, algorithms designed to minimize losses or capitalize on trends may inadvertently contribute to rapid price fluctuations.

Market transparency is another area that warrants attention. As AI algorithms become increasingly complex, their decision-making processes may become less understandable to human traders. This lack of transparency raises questions about accountability and the potential for unintended consequences in the financial markets.

Regulators are actively navigating the landscape of AI trading, working to strike a balance between fostering innovation and ensuring market integrity. As AI algorithms become integral to trading ecosystems, regulatory frameworks are evolving to address concerns related to fairness, accountability, and market stability.

In conclusion, AI trading algorithms represent a significant evolution in the financial markets. Their ability to process vast amounts of data, adapt to changing conditions, and manage risks positions them as a driving force in the future of trading. While challenges exist, ongoing developments in technology and regulation aim to harness the potential benefits of AI algorithms while mitigating associated risks. As these algorithms continue to shape the landscape of financial markets, staying informed about their capabilities and limitations will be essential for traders and investors alike.

Automated Stock Analysis Tools

In the fast-paced realm of stock markets, where every second counts, automated stock analysis tools empowered by artificial intelligence have emerged as indispensable allies for traders and investors. These tools not only process vast amounts of data at lightning speed but also utilize advanced algorithms to uncover trends, patterns, and insights that might elude the human eye. In this essay, we delve into the landscape of automated stock analysis, exploring five trending AI tools that are reshaping the way financial markets are navigated.

1. AlphaSense: Navigating the Sea of Financial Information

Introduction to AlphaSense:

AlphaSense is an AI-powered platform designed to streamline the process of extracting relevant insights from an extensive range of financial documents, including earnings call transcripts, SEC filings, and news articles. Its natural language processing capabilities enable users to quickly access critical information that could impact stock prices.

Key Features:

- **Real-time search:** AlphaSense offers a real-time search functionality, allowing users to stay updated on market-moving events and news.

- **Sentiment analysis:** Understand market sentiment by analyzing the tone and context of financial documents, aiding in informed decision-making.

- **Smart synonyms:** The platform employs intelligent synonyms, ensuring users don't miss critical information due to variations in terminology.

2. Kensho: Forecasting Market Impact With Machine Intelligence

Introduction to Kensho:

Kensho, now a part of S&P Global, employs machine intelligence to analyze financial events and predict their potential impact on various asset classes. This AI tool is particularly adept at automating complex financial research and providing actionable insights for traders.

Key Features:

- **Event recognition:** Kensho excels in recognizing and analyzing events, from economic indicators to geopolitical developments, enabling traders to anticipate market movements.

- **Natural language query:** Users can interact with Kensho using natural language queries, making it accessible even for those without advanced technical expertise.

- **Scenario analysis:** Conduct scenario analysis based on potential market-moving events, allowing for proactive risk management.

3. Yewno|Edge: Uncovering Hidden Patterns and Connections

Introduction to Yewno|Edge:

Yewno|Edge employs machine learning and knowledge graphs to uncover hidden patterns, correlations, and emerging trends within vast datasets. This AI tool is designed to enhance investment research by providing a holistic understanding of interconnected information.

Key Features:

- **Graph-based visualization:** Yewno|Edge presents information in a visually intuitive graph format, aiding in the identification of relationships and dependencies.

- **Thematic investing:** Identify thematic investment opportunities by exploring connections between companies, industries, and macroeconomic factors.

- **Quantitative and qualitative insights:** The platform combines quantitative data with qualitative insights, offering a comprehensive view of potential investment opportunities.

4. Trade Ideas: AI-Driven Stock Discovery and Strategy Optimization

Introduction to Trade Ideas:

Trade Ideas leverages artificial intelligence to assist traders in discovering potential stocks and optimizing trading strategies. With a focus on real-time data and pattern recognition, this tool provides actionable insights for both novice and experienced traders.

Key Features:

- **Automated strategy creation:** Trade Ideas allows users to build and backtest automated trading strategies based on AI-driven pattern recognition.

- **Holly AI:** The platform's AI-powered virtual assistant, Holly, continuously scans the market for opportunities and provides alerts on potential trades.

- **Risk management:** Implement risk management parameters within trading strategies to enhance overall portfolio management.

5. Sentieo: Amplifying Research Capabilities With AI

Introduction to Sentieo:

Sentieo combines artificial intelligence with financial research, offering a comprehensive platform for investment professionals. From document search to data analytics, Sentieo streamlines the research process and enables users to make data-driven investment decisions.

Key Features:

- **Document search and analysis:** Sentieo's AI capabilities enhance document search, allowing users to quickly extract insights from financial documents and filings.

- **Data visualization:** Visualize and analyze financial data through customizable charts and graphs, aiding in trend identification and analysis.

- **Collaborative research:** The platform facilitates collaborative research, allowing teams to work seamlessly and share insights, enhancing collective decision-making.

Empowering Decisions in the Digital Stock Arena

As we traverse the digital landscape of stock markets, automated stock analysis tools fueled by artificial intelligence emerge as invaluable assets for traders and investors. AlphaSense, Kensho, Yewno|Edge, Trade Ideas, and Sentieo represent a glimpse into the transformative power of AI in decoding complex financial data. These tools not only enhance efficiency but also equip market participants with the analytical prowess needed to navigate the dynamic and unpredictable world of stocks.

The Rise of Automation in Stock Analysis

Traditionally, stock analysis involved intensive manual research and analysis. However, the advent of automated stock analysis tools has transformed this process, leveraging technology to sift through vast amounts of data, identify patterns, and provide actionable insights. These tools harness the power of artificial intelligence and machine learning to enhance decision-making in the financial markets.

Key Features of Automated Stock Analysis Tools

Data Processing and Analysis

Automated stock analysis tools excel in processing large datasets swiftly. They can analyze historical price movements, financial statements, and market indicators in real time providing a comprehensive overview of a stock's performance.

Technical Indicators and Chart Patterns

These tools leverage technical indicators and chart patterns to identify trends and potential entry or exit points. By automatically recognizing patterns that might be challenging for human analysis, these tools enhance the precision of stock predictions.

Sentiment Analysis

Some advanced tools incorporate sentiment analysis of news articles, social media, and financial reports. This allows investors to gauge market sentiment and make informed decisions based on broader market perceptions.

Risk Management

Automated stock analysis tools often come equipped with risk management features. They can assess portfolio risk, set stop-loss orders, and offer recommendations to optimize risk-adjusted returns.

Benefits of Automated Stock Analysis Tools

Efficiency and Time-Saving

By automating data collection and analysis, these tools significantly reduce the time required for stock research. Investors can access insights swiftly, enabling faster decision-making in dynamic market conditions.

Elimination of Emotional Bias

One of the primary advantages is the elimination of emotional biases in decision-making. Automated tools rely on data-driven insights, removing emotional responses that can often cloud judgment in stock trading.

Enhanced Accuracy

The precision and accuracy of predictions are heightened with automated tools. Machine learning algorithms continuously learn from data patterns, improving their forecasting capabilities over time.

Accessibility

Automated stock analysis tools offer accessibility to both seasoned investors and newcomers. With user-friendly interfaces and intuitive dashboards, investors can navigate complex financial data with ease.

Considerations and Challenges

While automation brings efficiency, overreliance on these tools without understanding underlying algorithms can pose risks. The "black-box" nature of some advanced models may limit investors' understanding of the decision-making process. As these tools process vast amounts of financial data, ensuring robust security measures to protect sensitive information is crucial. Investors must be cautious about the data privacy policies of the tools they choose. Automated tools may face challenges during periods of extreme market volatility. Unprecedented events or sudden market shifts can pose difficulties for algorithms that rely on historical patterns. Automated stock analysis tools represent a significant leap forward in the financial industry, providing investors with powerful tools to navigate the complexities of stock markets. While not without challenges, the benefits of enhanced efficiency, accuracy, and accessibility make these tools indispensable for those looking to make informed and strategic investment decisions. As technology continues to advance, the integration of automated stock analysis tools will likely play a pivotal role in shaping the future of financial markets.

E-Commerce Bots and Virtual Assistants

E-commerce has witnessed a surge in the integration of AI-powered chatbots to enhance customer engagement and satisfaction. Chatbot platforms such as Chatbot.com and MobileMonkey empower businesses to automate customer interactions, address queries, and even drive sales. For entrepreneurs in the e-commerce space, these chatbots serve as passive income generators by ensuring consistent customer support and potentially boosting sales. With just a few simple tools, you can also create your own chatbots for eager customers wanting to optimize their online shopping experience, where user experience reigns supreme. These intelligent tools not only enhance customer interactions but also streamline business processes. For beginners venturing into the world of e-commerce chatbot development, this essay explores a curated selection of AI tools that serve as invaluable companions on the journey to crafting efficient and engaging virtual assistants.

1. Dialogflow: Google's Conversational Powerhouse

Introduction to Dialogflow

Dialogflow, a Google Cloud product, stands as a pioneer in conversational AI, empowering developers to create robust chatbots and virtual assistants. With its natural language processing capabilities, Dialogflow understands user inputs, enabling seamless interactions.

Key Features for Beginners

- **User-friendly interface:** Dialogflow offers an intuitive interface for designing conversational flows, making it accessible for beginners.

- **Multi-language support:** Reach a global audience by building chatbots that understand and respond in multiple languages.

- **Integration capabilities:** Easily integrate Dialogflow with various messaging platforms, websites, and mobile apps.

2. Microsoft Bot Framework: Empowering Cross-Channel Experiences

Introduction to Microsoft Bot Framework

Microsoft Bot Framework provides a comprehensive set of tools and services for building conversational applications. Whether deployed on websites, Microsoft Teams, or other channels, this framework ensures a consistent and engaging user experience.

- **Bot building SDK:** The Bot Framework SDK simplifies the development process, allowing beginners to create bots using .NET or Node.js.

- **Adaptive cards:** Enhance the visual appeal of your chatbot by utilizing adaptive cards for interactive and dynamic content.

- **Azure integration:** Leverage Azure services for robust bot hosting, analytics, and cognitive services.

3. IBM Watson Assistant: Elevating Conversations With AI Prowess

Introduction to IBM Watson Assistant

IBM Watson Assistant brings the cognitive computing power of IBM Watson to the realm of chatbots. It enables developers to build AI-powered virtual assistants capable of understanding user intents and providing context-aware responses.

Key Features for Beginners

- **Intent recognition:** Watson Assistant excels in understanding user intents, allowing for more natural and contextually relevant conversations.

- **Easy deployment:** Beginners can swiftly deploy their chatbots on websites and messaging platforms and even integrate them into mobile applications.

- **Machine learning insights:** Leverage machine learning to gain insights into user interactions and continuously improve your chatbot's performance.

4. Chatfuel: Simplifying Chatbot Creation for Social Commerce

Introduction to Chatfuel

For e-commerce businesses looking to integrate chatbots seamlessly into social media platforms, Chatfuel offers a user-friendly platform tailored for creating chatbots on Facebook Messenger.

Key Features for Beginners

- **Visual chatbot builder:** Beginners can design chatbot flows using Chatfuel's drag-and-drop interface without delving into complex coding.

- **E-commerce templates:** Explore pre-built templates specifically crafted for e-commerce scenarios, facilitating quicker bot creation.

- **User segmentation:** Personalize interactions by segmenting users based on preferences, behaviors, or purchasing history.

5. Rasa: Open Source Flexibility for E-commerce Dialogue

Introduction to Rasa

For those inclined toward open-source solutions, Rasa stands out as a versatile platform for building AI-driven chatbots. It empowers developers to have complete control over their conversational agents.

Key Features for Beginners

- **Open source framework:** Enjoy the flexibility and transparency of an open-source framework, allowing customization to fit unique e-commerce needs.

- **NLU and dialogue management:** Rasa excels in natural language understanding (NLU) and dialogue management, ensuring contextual and coherent conversations.

- **Community support:** Engage with a vibrant community for guidance, best practices, and collaborative problem-solving.

Building Intelligent Bridges in E-Commerce Conversations

Embarking on the journey to create an e-commerce chatbot or virtual assistant can be both exciting and rewarding for beginners. With tools like Dialogflow, Microsoft Bot Framework, IBM Watson Assistant, Chatfuel, and Rasa, the process becomes not only accessible but also tailored to the unique needs of e-commerce. These AI companions pave the way for more engaging, efficient, and personalized customer interactions, ultimately fostering growth and success in the dynamic world of online commerce.

Unleashing AI in Social Media Marketing: A Paradigm Shift

Understanding Audience Behavior With AI Analytics

AI has bestowed marketers with the power to decipher intricate patterns in user behavior. Advanced analytics tools, such as those driven by machine learning algorithms, dissect vast amounts of social media data. These insights delve beyond mere likes and shares, providing a nuanced understanding of user preferences, posting times, and content resonance. Armed with this knowledge, marketers can tailor their strategies with surgical precision, ensuring each post resonates with the intended audience.

Automated Content Curation and Generation

Efficiency meets creativity as AI takes the reins in content creation. Platforms leveraging natural language processing (NLP) and machine learning algorithms can curate engaging content tailored to specific audiences. From generating catchy captions to suggesting trending hashtags, AI streamlines the content creation process. It doesn't replace human creativity; rather, it complements it by offering data-backed suggestions and freeing up valuable time for marketers to focus on strategy and brand narrative.

Artificial intelligence has emerged as a powerful ally for writers, marketers, and businesses seeking to streamline their content generation processes. Among the myriad AI-driven platforms, JasperDocs and WritesonicAI stand out as wizards crafting compelling, engaging, and tailored content. This chapter delves into the functionalities of these platforms and provides a comprehensive guide on how beginners can harness their capabilities to elevate their content creation game.

Understanding JasperDocs

Introduction to JasperDocs

JasperDocs is a cutting-edge AI document generation platform designed to simplify the often intricate process of creating documents. Powered by advanced natural language processing algorithms, JasperDocs transforms raw data into coherent, professionally formatted documents across various industries.

How to Use JasperDocs

1. **Sign-up and profile creation**

   o Begin your JasperDocs journey by signing up for an account.

   o Create a profile specifying your industry and document requirements to tailor the AI's suggestions to your needs.

2. **Input data and preferences**

   o Feed JasperDocs with the raw data you want to include in your document.

   o Specify your preferences regarding formatting, tone, and style to ensure the output aligns with your unique voice.

3. **AI-powered document generation**

   o Let JasperDocs work its magic. The AI algorithms analyze your input, generating a draft document with coherent structure and language.

   o Explore customization options to fine-tune the document to meet your specific requirements.

4. **Edit and refine**

   o Review the generated document and make any necessary edits or refinements.

   o Utilize JasperDocs' collaboration features to gather feedback from colleagues or clients.

5. **Download and share**

   ○ Once satisfied, download the final document in your preferred format.

   ○ Easily share the professionally crafted content across various platforms.

Elevating Your Copywriting Game With AI Brilliance

Introduction to WritesonicAI

WritesonicAI positions itself as a game-changer in the realm of copywriting, offering AI-driven content creation tools tailored for marketers, entrepreneurs, and writers. Whether you need catchy headlines, persuasive ad copy, or engaging blog content, WritesonicAI leverages advanced algorithms to deliver results.

How to Use WritesonicAI

1. **Account setup and profile configuration**

   ○ Kickstart your WritesonicAI experience by creating an account.

   ○ Configure your profile by specifying your industry, tone preferences, and content goals.

2. **Select a writing tool**

   ○ Navigate through WritesonicAI's suite of writing tools, each designed for specific content needs.

- Choose from options like "AI Article," "Copywriting Assistant," or "Blog Ideas" based on your current project.

3. **Input prompts and customize**

- Input prompts or brief descriptions of the content you're seeking.

- Leverage customization options to define your writing style, tone, and desired length.

4. **AI-generated content**

- Let WritesonicAI's algorithms generate content based on your prompts and preferences.

- Explore multiple suggestions and variations to find the perfect fit for your requirements.

5. **Edit and optimize**

- Review the AI-generated content and make any necessary edits or optimizations.

- Utilize the platform's editing features to ensure the output aligns seamlessly with your brand voice.

6. **Download and deploy**

- Download the final copy in your preferred format.

- Deploy AI-crafted content across your marketing channels, websites, or social media platforms.

Comparative Strengths and Unique Features

JasperDocs

- **Document precision:** JasperDocs excels in crafting detailed and structured documents, making it ideal for industries requiring meticulous documentation.

- **Collaboration features:** The platform facilitates seamless collaboration, allowing multiple users to contribute to and refine documents.

WritesonicAI

- **Copywriting brilliance:** WritesonicAI specializes in copywriting, offering a suite of tools tailored for crafting persuasive and engaging content.

- **Versatility:** From blog ideas to ad copy, WritesonicAI provides a range of tools, offering versatility for various content needs.

In the dynamic landscape of content creation, JasperDocs and WritesonicAI emerge as indispensable allies for individuals and businesses alike. Whether you're striving for meticulously crafted documents or seeking captivating copy to captivate your audience, these AI wizards offer the tools to transform your content creation process. By understanding their functionalities and following the beginner's guide provided, you can harness the power of JasperDocs and WritesonicAI to elevate your content game with precision and brilliance.

Chatbots: Elevating Customer Interaction

In the realm of customer service, AI-driven chatbots have emerged as invaluable assets. These intelligent virtual assistants engage with users in real time, answering queries, providing information, and even facilitating transactions. Integrating chatbots into social media platforms ensures round-the-clock availability, enhancing user experience and fostering a sense of immediate interaction. This not only satisfies user queries promptly but also contributes to building a responsive and customer-centric brand image.

Predictive Analytics for Campaign Optimization

The success of social media campaigns relies on strategic decisions. Here, predictive analytics fueled by AI plays a pivotal role. By analyzing historical data and user behavior, predictive models forecast the potential outcomes of different campaign strategies. Marketers can optimize their approach by allocating resources to the channels, content types, and posting schedules with the highest probability of success. This not only enhances campaign performance but also ensures a more efficient allocation of resources.

More AI Tools and Platforms

Hootsuite: Orchestrating Social Media Management

Hootsuite, powered by AI, stands as a stalwart companion for social media managers. Its AI capabilities include content scheduling, performance tracking, and even suggesting optimal posting times. By automating mundane tasks, Hootsuite allows marketers to focus on crafting compelling content and refining their overall strategy.

Buffer: Crafting a Seamless Posting Experience

Buffer, another noteworthy AI-driven tool, simplifies the process of managing multiple social media accounts. With features like content scheduling, performance analytics, and audience engagement insights, Buffer ensures that marketers maintain a consistent and impactful online presence.

Canva: AI-Infused Design Brilliance

In the visual-centric world of social media, Canva stands out as an AI-infused design powerhouse. Its algorithms assist users in creating visually stunning graphics, ensuring that even those without a design background can produce eye-catching content. Canva's AI analyzes design trends, suggesting layouts, color palettes, and elements that align with current preferences.

Joining the AI-Driven Social Media Revolution: Key Communities

Stack Overflow: A Haven for Social Media AI Enthusiasts

Social media marketers delving into AI can find a wealth of knowledge on platforms like Stack Overflow. Engaging in discussions related to social media AI tools, algorithms, and case studies provides valuable insights and solutions to common challenges.

LinkedIn Groups: Nurturing AI-Driven Social Media Discussions

LinkedIn groups focused on AI in social media serve as vibrant hubs for professionals seeking to expand their knowledge. By participating in discussions, sharing experiences, and staying updated on industry trends, marketers can tap into collective wisdom and foster meaningful connections.

AI Webinars and Conferences: Immersive Learning Opportunities

Participating in AI-centric webinars and conferences offers an immersive learning experience. Events like the AI Summit and industry-specific webinars provide a platform to connect with experts, gain insights into emerging trends, and stay at the forefront of AI's integration into social media marketing.

The fusion of AI and social media marketing is a dynamic evolution that empowers marketers to navigate the complexities of the digital landscape. By embracing AI tools and platforms and engaging with AI communities, marketers can harness the full potential of this transformative synergy, creating campaigns that resonate, engage, and drive unprecedented success.

AI Tools for Website Creation

In the fast-evolving landscape of website creation, AI tools have emerged as game-changers, simplifying the process and empowering individuals and businesses to craft compelling online presences with minimal effort. This chapter explores two prominent AI-driven website builders—Zyro and Wix ADI. By understanding how to leverage these tools effectively, users can harness the power of AI to design, customize, and launch professional-looking websites effortlessly.

Zyro: Streamlined Website Building

Zyro is a user-friendly website builder that integrates artificial intelligence to streamline the design process. Upon initiating the website creation journey, Zyro prompts users with a set of questions related to their industry, preferences, and specific needs. The AI algorithm then generates a tailored template, suggesting layouts, color schemes, and content structures based on the provided information.

Using Zyro for Effortless Website Creation

1. **Initiate the website-building process**. Begin by signing up for a Zyro account. Once logged in, select the option to create a new website. Zyro's AI-driven system will guide you

through a series of questions to understand your goals and preferences.

2. **Customize the generated design**. After the AI generates a preliminary design based on your inputs, explore customization options. Adjust the color scheme, fonts, and layout to align with your brand identity. Zyro provides intuitive tools that allow for easy modifications without delving into intricate design details.

3. **Content integration and enhancement**. Zyro simplifies content integration by suggesting sections and content elements based on your industry and goals. Enhance these suggestions by adding your unique text, images, and multimedia components. The AI algorithm adapts the layout dynamically as you input content, ensuring a cohesive and professional appearance.

4. **Preview and launch**. Once satisfied with the design and content, preview your website to see how it will appear to visitors. Zyro's real-time preview feature allows you to make final adjustments. When ready, hit the launch button to publish your website to the web.

Wix ADI: AI-Powered Design Assistant

Wix ADI, part of the renowned Wix website builder, stands as an AI-powered design assistant dedicated to simplifying the website creation process. Users start by answering a series of questions about their objectives, style preferences, and features they desire. Wix ADI then employs this data to generate a personalized website design, complete with content suggestions and an optimized layout.

Harnessing Wix ADI for Seamless Website Development

1. **Begin the website-creation process**. Start by creating a Wix account if you don't have one. Choose to create a new website and opt for the Wix ADI option. Provide information about your website's purpose, features you want, and your preferred style. Wix ADI will use this data to generate a personalized design.

2. **Tailor the design to your liking**. Wix ADI generates a design template based on your inputs. Customize the design further by modifying colors, fonts, and layout elements. Wix's intuitive drag-and-drop editor allows for easy adjustments without the need for coding skills.

3. **Add and refine content**. Integrate your content into the generated structure. Wix ADI suggests content elements based on your initial inputs. Enhance these suggestions by adding your text, images, and multimedia components. Wix's platform offers robust content management tools for seamless editing.

4. **Preview and publish**. Preview your website to ensure it aligns with your vision. Wix provides a comprehensive preview feature that allows you to navigate through your site as visitors would. Once satisfied, hit the publish button to make your website live on the internet.

Comparing Zyro and Wix ADI

Zyro's Strengths and Unique Features

- **Simplicity:** Zyro excels in simplicity, making it an ideal choice for users seeking a straightforward and quick website creation process.

- **Affordability:** Zyro offers competitive pricing plans, making it budget-friendly for individuals and small businesses.

- **AI-powered design:** Zyro's AI designs are tailored based on user preferences, streamlining the creative process.

Wix ADI's Strengths and Unique Features

- **Design flexibility:** Wix ADI provides a high level of design flexibility, allowing users to fine-tune their website appearance according to specific preferences.

- **Extensive app market:** Wix boasts a rich app market, enabling users to integrate various functionalities and features seamlessly.

- **Diverse templates:** Wix offers a wide array of templates even within its ADI feature, providing diverse options for different industries.

Empowering Your Online Presence With AI Tools

As the digital landscape continues to evolve, leveraging AI tools like Zyro and Wix ADI becomes a strategic move for individuals and businesses aiming to establish a strong online presence. Whether you prioritize simplicity, affordability, or design flexibility, these AI-driven website builders offer valuable solutions for crafting visually appealing and functional websites with minimal effort.

These AI tools represent a snapshot of the diverse opportunities available for passive income generation in the current AI landscape. From financial markets to content creation and e-commerce, the integration of AI technologies empowers individuals to build income streams that operate autonomously, requiring minimal ongoing effort. As we navigate the intricacies of each tool, it becomes evident that the synergy between AI innovation and passive income potential is a defining feature of the contemporary digital landscape. The journey toward building a robust AI toolbox involves not only selecting the right tools but also understanding how they align with individual goals and strategies for passive income generation.

Chapter 4:

Creating Scalable AI Models

Given the nature of this book and its focus on AI, there are doubtless going to be readers who wield the wit and intellect to create their own AI models from first principles. Although this book doesn't aim to be a treatise in computer science, we will briefly go over some operating principles for designing a robust and scalable AI model of your very own. We will also assume here that the reader has at least a rudimentary understanding and familiarity with the Python programming language.

Please also keep in mind that trading algorithms most commonly run on the PineScript coding language, so when developing an AI for deployment in live markets, an API will be required to excuse the trades on the actual trading exchange, and another API or webhook can be used to communicate between the PineScript code and the AI algorithm developed in Python.

Principles in AI Model Creation for AI Model Design in Python

In the realm of artificial intelligence, the efficiency and scalability of models are pivotal elements that can make or break their real-world applicability. This section explores the fundamental principles guiding the creation of scalable AI models, catering specifically to individuals well-versed in the Python programming language.

Understanding Scalability in AI

Scalability in the context of AI models refers to the ability of a system to handle increased workloads smoothly. For Python enthusiasts diving into the AI sphere, it's crucial to comprehend scalability not only in terms of model performance but also concerning computational resources, data handling, and deployment.

Data Preprocessing and Pipelines

Efficient data preprocessing lays the foundation for scalable AI models. Python's extensive libraries, such as Pandas and NumPy, provide powerful tools for data manipulation and transformation. Adopting well-structured data pipelines ensures a streamlined process, enabling scalability by facilitating easy integration of additional data sources.

Model Architecture Design

Scalability considerations should be embedded in the very architecture of AI models. Python frameworks like TensorFlow and PyTorch offer modular design principles. Building models as modular components allows for easy scalability by replacing or adding modules as the complexity of the task or the dataset size increases.

Parallel Processing and Distributed Computing

Python's multiprocessing and parallel computing capabilities are instrumental in achieving scalability. Leveraging libraries like Dask or Joblib allows the distribution of computations across multiple cores, enhancing model training speed and accommodating larger datasets. For more extensive scalability demands, transitioning to distributed computing frameworks like Apache Spark becomes essential.

Feature Engineering for Flexibility

Python's rich ecosystem of machine learning libraries enables feature engineering that enhances model adaptability and scalability. Feature selection and extraction methods can be employed to handle varying data dimensions efficiently. This ensures that models remain scalable across diverse datasets without compromising performance.

Optimizing Model Training With Generators

In the quest for scalable AI models, the memory efficiency of Python becomes a crucial consideration. Implementing generators in data processing and model training allows the handling of extensive datasets without consuming excessive memory. This approach is particularly advantageous when dealing with large-scale datasets that cannot fit into RAM.

Containerization for Portability

Containerization technologies like Docker have gained popularity for deploying scalable AI models. Packaging models and their dependencies into containers ensures consistency across different environments, streamlining the deployment process. Python's compatibility with containerization tools aligns seamlessly with the scalability needs of diverse applications.

Integration of Cloud Services

Python's interoperability with cloud service providers, such as AWS, Azure, or Google Cloud, opens doors to scalable AI solutions. Cloud-based solutions offer on-demand computational resources, enabling Python enthusiasts to scale their models effortlessly based on varying workloads.

Scalability involves not only efficient model training but also seamless deployment and versioning. Python frameworks like Flask and FastAPI provide robust solutions for deploying scalable AI models as APIs. Implementing strategies like blue-green deployment ensures continuous availability during updates or scalability adjustments.

Monitoring and Auto-scaling in Production

Once an AI model is deployed, real-world scalability comes into play. Leveraging Python-compatible monitoring tools, such as Prometheus or Grafana, allows continuous performance evaluation. Incorporating auto-scaling mechanisms ensures that deployed models can dynamically adapt to fluctuations in usage, maintaining optimal responsiveness.

Embarking on the journey of creating scalable AI models with Python as your compass requires a meticulous understanding of the interplay between data, algorithms, and computational resources. Navigating through data preprocessing, modular architecture, parallel processing, and deployment strategies equips Python enthusiasts with the tools to harness scalability effectively. As the realms of AI and Python continue to evolve, embracing these principles ensures that your AI endeavors not only perform efficiently but also scale gracefully to meet the demands of an ever-evolving landscape.

Designing AI Models for Scalability and Growth

In the ever-expanding seas of artificial intelligence, the journey doesn't end with the creation of a scalable model; it extends into the uncharted territories of designing models with scalability and sustained growth in mind. Building upon the principles laid out in the previous section, this exploration navigates the strategic aspects of AI model design to ensure they not only scale gracefully but also evolve in tandem with the dynamic demands of the AI landscape.

Adaptive Model Architecture

Designing AI models for sustained growth involves crafting architectures that can evolve over time. Python's flexibility in model design, especially with dynamic frameworks like PyTorch, allows for the integration of adaptive components. Future-proofing models involve anticipating changes in input dimensions, task complexity, or the emergence of new data sources.

Python's machine learning libraries, such as TensorFlow and Keras, empower practitioners to implement transfer learning effectively. By designing models with transferable knowledge in mind, future iterations can leverage pre-trained components, facilitating continuous learning and adaptation to new tasks. This approach is particularly valuable in scenarios where labeled data is scarce.

Dynamic Hyperparameter Tuning

Python enthusiasts can harness the power of libraries like scikit-learn to implement dynamic hyperparameter tuning. Designing models with tunable parameters allows for fine-tuning as new data reveals optimal configurations. This adaptability ensures that AI models remain effective and efficient as they encounter diverse datasets or face varying computational constraints.

Incorporating Feedback Loops

Scalability and growth are inherently linked to feedback loops. Python's integration with reinforcement learning libraries enables the incorporation of feedback mechanisms. Designing models with the ability to learn from ongoing interactions ensures adaptability to changes in user preferences, environment dynamics, or evolving objectives. As AI models grow, training pipelines must scale efficiently. Python's support for scalable distributed computing frameworks, like Apache Spark or TensorFlow Extended (TFX), facilitates the creation of training pipelines that can handle increasing data volumes and complexities. The design should accommodate not only current scalability needs but also the potential for future expansion.

Designing AI models for sustained growth requires an understanding of the importance of model interpretability. Python's libraries, like SHAP or LIME, provide tools to interpret complex models. Ensuring models are interpretable aids in debugging, refinement, and adaptability, especially when faced with evolving business requirements or regulatory changes. The AI landscape is dynamic, witnessing the emergence of novel architectures like transformers or GPT models. Python's extensibility allows practitioners to integrate these advancements into existing models seamlessly. Designing models with compatibility for cutting-edge architectures ensures that they remain relevant and competitive in the evolving AI ecosystem.

Python's vibrant community contributes to a myriad of AI-related projects. Designing models with modularity and compatibility encourages community-driven enhancements. Leveraging open-source contributions allows models to benefit from ongoing improvements, extending their life cycle and adaptability. Growth in AI applications often invites increased attention from potential threats. Designing models with robust security measures becomes paramount. Python's ecosystem offers tools for secure model deployment, encryption, and monitoring. An integrated approach to security ensures that models can scale without compromising data integrity or user privacy.

Agile Deployment Strategies

Python frameworks like Flask or FastAPI enable agile deployment strategies. Designing models with deployability in mind ensures that they can be seamlessly integrated into evolving infrastructures. The ability to deploy models swiftly facilitates rapid iterations, incorporating improvements and adaptations driven by changing requirements.

In the vast and ever-evolving landscape of AI, the design of models must transcend mere scalability; it should embrace growth, adaptability, and continuous learning. Python, with its versatile ecosystem, empowers practitioners to design models that not only navigate the currents of current challenges but also set sail confidently toward the horizons of future possibilities.

Automation Strategies

The best method for automating your workflow for passive income is through the use of APIs. These were mentioned at the beginning of the chapter, and they are absolutely crucial to earning passively through AI. It is the APIs that enable the programs to communicate with each other and automate the work you would have otherwise had to personally attend to. More so than coding your own AI, as glorious as that may sound, coding APIs that build a bridge of communication between various AIs is a more effective use of you time as opposed to reinventing the wheel by attempting to build and scale a model from scratch. APIs act as intermediaries that enable different software components to interact. They define a set of rules and protocols specifying how software components should communicate. APIs facilitate the exchange of data and functionalities between applications without requiring the user to delve into the internal workings of each system.

Significance of APIs in Automation

1. **Efficiency and productivity:** APIs enable the automation of repetitive tasks by providing a standardized way for applications to communicate. This reduces manual intervention, enhancing overall efficiency and productivity.

2. **Data integration:** APIs allow disparate systems to share and synchronize data seamlessly. This is particularly valuable in scenarios where data from one application is needed in another, eliminating the need for manual data entry.

3. **Scalability:** Automation powered by APIs is inherently scalable. As business needs evolve, additional functionalities can be integrated into existing workflows through API connections.

4. **Real-time communication:** APIs facilitate real-time data exchange, ensuring that information is up-to-date across all connected systems. This is vital for scenarios where timely data is critical for decision-making.

Practical Applications of API-Driven Automation

1. **Social media management:** Tools like the Facebook Graph API or Twitter API enable businesses to automate social media posting, analyze engagement metrics, and respond to customer interactions programmatically.

2. **E-commerce integration:** APIs play a pivotal role in connecting e-commerce platforms with payment gateways,

inventory management systems, and shipping services. This integration streamlines the entire e-commerce workflow.

3. **Cloud service automation:** Cloud providers offer APIs for automating resource provisioning, scaling, and monitoring. This is indispensable for organizations leveraging cloud infrastructure.

4. **Workflow orchestration:** APIs are used to orchestrate complex workflows involving multiple applications. Automation platforms leverage APIs to ensure seamless coordination between different tasks.

Best Practices for API-Driven Workflow Automation

1. **API documentation:** Thoroughly understand the documentation of the APIs you intend to use. Comprehensive documentation provides insights into available endpoints, request methods, and expected responses.

2. **Authentication and security:** Implement robust authentication mechanisms, such as API keys or OAuth, to secure API connections. Regularly update credentials and adhere to security best practices.

3. **Error Handling:** Design automated workflows with robust error-handling mechanisms. APIs may return errors, and a well-constructed automation script should gracefully manage such scenarios.

4. **Rate limiting:** Respect rate limits imposed by APIs to prevent service disruptions. Monitoring API usage and adjusting workflows accordingly ensures adherence to service provider guidelines.

APIs serve as the backbone of workflow automation, fostering seamless integration between diverse applications. Embracing APIs for automation enhances efficiency, enables data-driven decision-making, and positions organizations to thrive in the ever-evolving digital landscape. As businesses continue to navigate the complexities of a connected world, API-driven workflow automation emerges as a transformative force, empowering organizations to achieve new heights of productivity and innovation.

Predictive Modeling in Different Industries

AI has revolutionized predictive modeling across various industries, fundamentally altering the landscape of decision-making and forecasting. This section explores the profound impact of AI on predictive modeling and its diverse applications.

In the realm of finance, AI has ushered in a new era of predictive modeling, enhancing risk assessment and investment strategies. Traditional financial models often struggle to adapt to dynamic market conditions. However, AI-driven predictive models, fueled by machine learning algorithms, can analyze vast datasets in real time, discerning complex patterns and market trends. This capability empowers financial institutions to make more informed decisions, mitigate risks, and optimize investment portfolios.

Similarly, healthcare has witnessed a transformative shift in predictive modeling with the integration of AI. Machine learning algorithms, when fed with extensive patient data, can predict disease outbreaks, identify potential health risks, and optimize treatment plans. Predictive modeling in healthcare aids in early diagnosis, personalized medicine, and resource allocation, ultimately improving patient outcomes and the efficiency of healthcare systems.

In manufacturing, AI has played a pivotal role in predictive maintenance. Traditional maintenance schedules were often based on fixed intervals or reactive responses to equipment failures. AI-driven predictive models leverage sensor data and historical performance metrics to forecast potential equipment failures. This proactive approach minimizes downtime, reduces maintenance costs, and ensures optimal operational efficiency.

The retail sector has harnessed the power of AI to revolutionize demand forecasting and inventory management. Predictive modeling powered by AI algorithms analyzes consumer behavior, market trends, and external factors in real time. Retailers can optimize their inventory levels, prevent stockouts or overstock situations, and enhance the overall supply chain efficiency.

In the energy sector, AI has been instrumental in predictive modeling for energy consumption and distribution. Machine learning algorithms analyze historical energy usage patterns, weather conditions, and other relevant data to predict future demand. This allows energy providers to optimize resource allocation, reduce wastage, and enhance the sustainability of energy distribution.

The field of marketing has witnessed a paradigm shift in customer relationship management and targeted advertising due to AI-driven predictive modeling. Analyzing customer behavior, preferences, and engagement patterns, AI algorithms can predict future trends, enabling businesses to tailor marketing strategies for maximum impact. Predictive modeling in marketing enhances customer acquisition and retention, contributing to overall business success.

While AI has undeniably revolutionized predictive modeling, it comes with its set of challenges and ethical considerations. The "black box" nature of some AI algorithms raises concerns about transparency and accountability. Bias in data, if not carefully addressed, can perpetuate and even exacerbate existing inequalities. Striking a balance between harnessing the power of AI for predictive modeling and ensuring ethical practices remains a crucial aspect of its continued integration across industries.

AI has reshaped predictive modeling across diverse industries, providing unprecedented insights, efficiency, and accuracy. From finance to healthcare, manufacturing to retail, and energy to marketing, the impact of AI-driven predictive modeling is both far-reaching and transformative. As technology continues to advance, the synergy between AI and predictive modeling will likely unlock new possibilities, revolutionizing decision-making processes and shaping the future of various industries.

Predictive Analytics: A Gateway to Passive Income Revolution

In the dynamic landscape of modern finance, individuals and businesses are increasingly turning to innovative technologies to unlock new streams of passive income. One such technological marvel that stands at the forefront is predictive analytics. This section delves into the realm of predictive analytics, exploring its fundamental principles, applications across diverse sectors, and how harnessing its power can pave the way for a passive income revolution.

Understanding Predictive Analytics

Predictive analytics involves the use of statistical algorithms and machine learning techniques to analyze historical data and forecast future trends. At its core, predictive analytics seeks to identify patterns, correlations, and hidden insights within vast datasets, enabling informed decision-making.

Principles of Predictive Analytics

Predictive analytics operates on the principles of extrapolation and pattern recognition. By identifying patterns in historical data, predictive models make educated guesses about future outcomes. These models continuously evolve as more data becomes available, enhancing their accuracy over time.

Applications Across Industries

Predictive analytics finds applications across a spectrum of industries, revolutionizing how organizations operate and make strategic decisions.

Financial markets

- In the realm of finance, predictive analytics plays a pivotal role in algorithmic trading. Trading algorithms leverage predictive models to analyze market trends, identify potential investment opportunities, and execute trades autonomously. This application has led to the emergence of automated trading platforms that generate passive income for users.

E-commerce and marketing

- E-commerce platforms utilize predictive analytics to personalize user experiences, recommend products, and optimize pricing strategies. Marketers leverage predictive models to identify target audiences, predict consumer behavior, and optimize advertising campaigns, contributing to passive income through increased sales and customer engagement.

Healthcare

- Predictive analytics is transforming healthcare by predicting disease outbreaks, identifying high-risk patients, and optimizing treatment plans. Remote patient monitoring and predictive diagnostics contribute to passive income generation by reducing healthcare costs and improving patient outcomes.

Real Estate

- In the real estate sector, predictive analytics aids in property valuation, market trend analysis, and identifying lucrative investment opportunities. Investors can harness predictive models to make informed decisions, leading to passive income through real estate appreciation and rental returns.

Human Resources

- Predictive analytics streamlines HR processes by forecasting employee turnover, identifying talent gaps, and optimizing recruitment strategies. Businesses can reduce hiring costs and enhance workforce efficiency, contributing to passive income through improved operational efficiency.

Predictive Analytics for Passive Income Generation:

Predictive analytics offers a myriad of opportunities for individuals seeking passive income streams.

Algorithmic trading platforms

- Individuals can leverage algorithmic trading platforms that harness predictive analytics to execute trades automatically based on predefined criteria. These platforms analyze market data, identify trends, and execute trades in real time, potentially generating passive income through optimized trading strategies.

Predictive content creation

- Content creators can utilize predictive analytics tools to analyze audience behavior, identify trending topics, and tailor content strategies. By creating content aligned with predictive insights, creators enhance their online visibility and audience engagement, leading to passive income through ad revenue and sponsorships.

E-commerce optimization

- Entrepreneurs in the e-commerce space can employ predictive analytics to optimize pricing strategies, manage inventory efficiently, and enhance the overall customer experience. This can result in increased sales and customer retention, contributing to passive income for e-commerce businesses.

Real Estate Investment

- Predictive analytics aids real estate investors in identifying high-potential properties, predicting market trends, and optimizing investment portfolios. Investors can capitalize on predictive insights to make strategic real estate decisions, leading to passive income through property appreciation and rental yields.

Affiliate marketing strategies

- Affiliates can leverage predictive analytics to identify high-converting products, optimize marketing channels, and tailor strategies based on consumer behavior trends. By aligning marketing efforts with predictive insights, affiliates can enhance passive income through commission-based earnings.

Challenges and Considerations

While predictive analytics holds immense potential for passive income generation, it's crucial to acknowledge the associated challenges and considerations.

Data privacy and security

- Predictive analytics relies on vast datasets, raising concerns about data privacy and security. Individuals and businesses must implement robust measures to protect sensitive information and adhere to regulatory frameworks.

Model accuracy and interpretability:

- The accuracy and interpretability of predictive models are critical. Overly complex models may hinder understanding, leading to suboptimal decision-making. Striking a balance between accuracy and interpretability is essential.

Continuous learning and adaptation:

- Predictive models require continuous learning and adaptation. Staying abreast of evolving trends, updating models, and incorporating new data are essential to maintaining their effectiveness.

Predictive analytics stands as a beacon of innovation, offering individuals and businesses the tools to navigate an era of passive income possibilities. From algorithmic trading to personalized content creation, the applications are diverse and transformative. As we embrace the predictive power of analytics, it's essential to tread carefully, addressing challenges and considering ethical implications. The journey toward a passive income revolution driven by predictive analytics is underway, inviting those willing to harness its potential to embark on a transformative financial odyssey.

Chapter 5:

Data

As with the previous chapter, some rudimentary knowledge of data analytics will be assumed for this chapter. Excel VBA is a great example that illustrates the monumental technological leap presented by AI in data analytics. In the same way that someone first being introduced to Excel manually enters each individual formula into each cell when processing a dataset, someone who is more familiar with Microsoft Excel might opt to automatically enter and alter these formulas on the back end by conditionally coding them into the cells using Excel VBA. A higher level of organization beyond that using an algorithm to optimize the formulae deployed by Excel VBA is the realm of AI analytics.

In the contemporary digital landscape, data has emerged as a formidable asset, and organizations are increasingly exploring innovative avenues to monetize the vast repositories they accumulate. The integration of AI into data monetization strategies has ushered in a new era of opportunities. This essay delves into the burgeoning trends of data monetization, exploring how AI is shaping these trends and highlighting examples of software that play pivotal roles in this evolving landscape.

Understanding Data Monetization

Data monetization involves converting raw data into revenue-generating opportunities. Organizations leverage their data assets by either directly selling information or using insights derived from data to enhance products, services, or decision-making processes. The intersection of AI and data monetization has proven transformative, enabling more sophisticated analysis, prediction, and automation.

Trends in Data Monetization Using AI

1. **Personalization paradigm:** AI-driven personalization stands out as a prominent trend in data monetization. By leveraging machine learning algorithms, organizations can analyze user behavior, preferences, and historical data to deliver personalized experiences. This trend is visible in content recommendations, targeted advertising, and product suggestions across various industries. Example software: Netflix employs AI algorithms to analyze viewing habits and preferences, offering personalized content recommendations to enhance user engagement.

2. **Predictive analytics for business insights:** Predictive analytics, powered by AI, is instrumental in extracting actionable insights from large datasets. Businesses utilize predictive models to forecast trends, identify potential risks, and optimize decision-making processes. This trend not only enhances operational efficiency but also opens avenues for monetizing predictive insights. Example software: Salesforce Einstein Analytics uses AI to analyze customer data, providing predictive insights that empower businesses to make informed decisions and drive revenue.

3. **AI in E-commerce and recommendation engines:** E-commerce platforms leverage AI to drive sales through recommendation engines. By analyzing user browsing history, purchase behavior, and demographic data, recommendation engines predict products of interest, increasing the likelihood of conversion. This trend has significant implications for revenue generation in the retail sector. Example software: Amazon's recommendation engine employs AI algorithms to suggest products based on user preferences, driving personalized shopping experiences and increasing sales.

4. **Monetizing IoT data:** The proliferation of the Internet of Things (IoT) has led to the generation of vast amounts of data from connected devices. AI plays a crucial role in extracting meaningful insights from IoT data, creating opportunities for monetization. Industries such as healthcare, smart cities, and manufacturing can leverage AI to derive value from IoT-generated data. Example software: IBM Watson IoT applies AI to analyze data from connected devices, offering insights that enable businesses to optimize operations and create new revenue streams.

5. **Enhanced customer engagement through chatbots:** AI-powered chatbots contribute to improved customer engagement and support services. Organizations deploy chatbots to interact with users, answer queries, and provide assistance. The data generated from these interactions can be monetized by understanding customer needs and preferences. Example software: Chatbot platforms like Drift and Intercom utilize AI to engage with users in real time, offering personalized interactions and gathering valuable data for monetization purposes.

Challenges and Considerations

While the integration of AI into data monetization brings forth lucrative opportunities, it is essential to navigate associated challenges:

1. **Data privacy and ethics:** Monetizing data necessitates a vigilant approach to data privacy and ethical considerations. Organizations must adhere to stringent privacy regulations and ensure transparent practices to maintain trust with users.

2. **Security concerns:** With the increasing volume of data transactions, security becomes paramount. AI-driven data monetization strategies should incorporate robust security

measures to safeguard sensitive information from potential breaches.

3. **Bias in AI algorithms:** AI algorithms may inadvertently perpetuate biases present in training data. Organizations need to address bias concerns to ensure fair and equitable data monetization practices. Data monetization, fueled by the capabilities of AI, is reshaping how organizations derive value from their data reservoirs. The trends highlighted—from personalization and predictive analytics to IoT data monetization—underscore the diverse opportunities that AI brings to the forefront. As businesses embark on this data-driven journey, it is crucial to balance innovation with ethical considerations, ensuring that the monetization of data aligns with privacy standards and societal expectations.

In this era where data is a prized commodity, the marriage of AI and data monetization stands as a testament to the transformative power of technology in driving economic value and innovation.

Ethical Concerns Over Data Acquisition

1. **Privacy concerns:** One of the foremost ethical considerations in data collection pertains to privacy. AI-driven technologies, ranging from facial recognition to predictive analytics, often involve the processing of personal information. Striking a balance between harnessing the potential of AI and safeguarding individual privacy remains a complex challenge. Illustrative case: The use of facial recognition in public spaces, such as surveillance cameras equipped with AI, raises concerns about unwarranted intrusion into individuals' private lives.

2. **Informed consent:** Obtaining informed consent is a cornerstone of ethical data collection. AI systems often rely on vast datasets, and individuals may not be fully aware of the extent to which their data is being utilized. Ensuring transparent communication and allowing individuals to make informed decisions about data usage is essential. Case study: Social media platforms face scrutiny for their data collection practices, where users may not be fully aware of how their information is utilized for targeted advertising or algorithmic content recommendations.

3. **Algorithmic bias and fairness:** The development and deployment of AI algorithms introduce the risk of bias, which can perpetuate existing inequalities. Biased algorithms may lead to discriminatory outcomes, affecting individuals based on factors such as race, gender, or socioeconomic status. Notable example: AI-driven hiring platforms have faced criticism for exhibiting bias in their selection processes, potentially perpetuating existing gender or racial disparities in employment.

4. **Transparency and explainability:** The opacity of AI algorithms poses challenges for transparency and accountability. Ethical data collection demands that individuals understand how their data is being used and have the ability to question and challenge algorithmic decisions. Case in point: Financial institutions employing AI for credit scoring should provide clear explanations of the factors influencing credit decisions to maintain transparency and trust.

5. **Data security and minimization:** Ensuring the security of collected data is integral to ethical considerations. Organizations must implement robust measures to protect against data breaches and unauthorized access. Additionally,

practicing data minimization—collecting only the necessary information for a specific purpose—aligns with privacy principles. Real-world scenario: Healthcare organizations utilizing AI for patient data analysis must prioritize data security to prevent unauthorized access to sensitive medical information.

6. **Societal impact and accountability:** The societal implications of widespread data collection through AI extend beyond individual concerns. Ethical considerations include accountability for the broader impact of data-driven technologies on communities, societies, and democratic processes. Examining the impact: Social media platforms face scrutiny for their role in disseminating misinformation and shaping public opinion, prompting discussions about the accountability of tech companies for societal outcomes.

7. **Cross-border data flow and global standards:** With data often transcending geographical boundaries, ethical considerations encompass issues of cross-border data flow and the lack of standardized global regulations. Ensuring that data collection practices align with ethical principles across diverse jurisdictions is a complex endeavor. Global dilemma: Companies operating internationally must navigate varying data protection laws, highlighting the need for global standards to govern ethical data collection practices.

Ethical considerations in data collection using AI form a critical aspect of responsible technological advancement. As AI continues to permeate various facets of our lives, from healthcare and finance to law enforcement and entertainment, addressing these ethical concerns becomes imperative.

Balancing innovation with ethical safeguards requires a concerted effort from policymakers, technologists, and society at large. Establishing clear regulations, fostering transparency, promoting responsible AI development, and prioritizing individual rights can collectively contribute to an ethical framework for data collection in the age of AI.

Building Profitable Data Sets

The importance of high-quality datasets cannot be overstated. The process of building a profitable dataset is a strategic endeavor that involves thoughtful planning, diverse data sources, and leveraging the capabilities of programming languages like Python. This essay explores the key principles and methodologies for constructing datasets that not only empower AI models but also contribute to profitable outcomes.

1. **Defining a profitable dataset:** A profitable dataset is one that aligns with the objectives of the AI application it serves. Whether the goal is predictive analytics, image recognition, or natural language processing, understanding the specific requirements and desired outcomes is fundamental. Profitability, in this context, may refer to the effectiveness of the dataset in enhancing model accuracy and efficiency or generating actionable insights.

2. **Identifying data sources:** The foundation of a profitable dataset lies in the diversity and relevance of its sources. Combining data from various channels—structured databases, unstructured text, images, and even sensor data—provides a holistic view that enriches the dataset. Accessing relevant external datasets or APIs further enhances the breadth and depth of information.

3. **Data quality and preprocessing:** Ensuring the quality of data is paramount. Cleaning and preprocessing steps, often performed using Python libraries, address issues like missing values, outliers, or inconsistencies. A profitable dataset hinges on the accuracy and reliability of its components, making thorough preprocessing an indispensable stage.

4. **Feature engineering:** Crafting meaningful features from raw data amplifies the dataset's efficacy. Python's versatility in handling data manipulation and transformation allows practitioners to create features that capture essential patterns and relationships. Effective feature engineering contributes to the model's ability to discern relevant information.

5. **Balancing and sampling:** Addressing class imbalances or skewed distributions is crucial for predictive models. Python's scikit-learn library provides tools for sampling techniques, ensuring a balanced representation of different classes. A profitable dataset optimally reflects the diversity of scenarios the AI model is expected to encounter.

6. **Temporal considerations:** Depending on the application, datasets may exhibit temporal patterns. Incorporating time-based features or considering the temporal evolution of data enhances the dataset's adaptability to changing conditions. Python's Pandas library facilitates time-series data handling, contributing to the dataset's temporal robustness.

7. **Ethical and regulatory compliance:** Building a profitable dataset also involves ethical considerations and compliance with regulations. Python, with its robust ecosystem, enables the implementation of privacy measures, anonymization techniques, and adherence to data protection standards. Ethical data practices contribute to long-term profitability by mitigating risks associated with misuse or non-compliance.

8. **Continuous monitoring and updating:** Profitability is an ongoing pursuit. Establishing mechanisms for continuous monitoring and updating of datasets is essential. Python scripts or automated workflows can facilitate real-time checks for data quality, ensuring that the dataset remains relevant and effective in a dynamic environment.

9. **Documentation and transparency:** A profitable dataset is well-documented and transparent. Python's capabilities in generating documentation through tools like Sphinx contribute to maintaining a comprehensive record of dataset characteristics, sources, and preprocessing steps. Transparent documentation fosters collaboration and builds trust in the dataset's reliability.

10. **Collaboration and reproducibility:** Python's emphasis on collaboration and reproducibility aligns with the principles of building profitable datasets. Utilizing version control systems and tools like Jupyter Notebooks ensures that dataset creation processes are transparent, collaborative, and reproducible, essential attributes for maintaining profitability over time.

Building a profitable dataset is an intricate process that demands a nuanced understanding of AI objectives, data characteristics, and ethical considerations. Python, with its versatility and extensive libraries, provides a powerful toolkit for practitioners to navigate this process effectively. From data collection to preprocessing, feature engineering, and ongoing monitoring, the principles outlined in this essay underscore the multifaceted nature of constructing datasets that not only serve AI models but also contribute to sustained profitability.

Chapter 6:

Diversifying Income Streams

Identifying complementary income streams is a strategic approach to diversifying revenue sources and ensuring sustainability. This chapter delves into the strategies and methodologies for recognizing and harnessing complementary AI income streams, providing insights for individuals and businesses seeking to maximize their earnings in the AI domain.

1. **Understanding complementary AI income streams:** Complementary income streams in AI refer to diverse revenue sources that, when combined, create a robust and balanced portfolio. These streams often leverage distinct AI applications, industries, or business models to mitigate risks associated with dependence on a single source of income.

2. **Exploring AI applications across industries:** To identify complementary income streams, it's essential to explore AI applications across various industries. From healthcare and finance to marketing and manufacturing, AI technologies offer versatile solutions. Understanding the unique challenges and opportunities in different sectors allows for strategic positioning to tap into multiple income streams.

3. **Creating synergies between AI services:** Synergies between AI services can be a powerful driver for complementary income. For example, a business providing AI-driven data analytics may complement its services by integrating predictive modeling or natural language processing. This

integration not only expands the service portfolio but also attracts a broader clientele.

4. **Combining product and service offerings:** Developing a hybrid model that combines AI product and service offerings enhances income streams. Companies can create proprietary AI products while offering consulting, customization, and maintenance services. This diversification ensures revenue stability, balancing the potential fluctuations in product sales with consistent service-based income.

5. **Leveraging AI for content creation and monetization:** Content creation fueled by AI, including articles, videos, or design assets, can become a lucrative income stream. Platforms like OpenAI's GPT-3 enable the generation of high-quality content. By leveraging this content for marketing, advertising, or subscription-based models, individuals and businesses can tap into complementary AI-driven revenue.

6. **Exploring AI in e-commerce and personalization:** E-commerce businesses can benefit from AI-driven personalization, recommendation engines, and predictive analytics. Implementing AI technologies to enhance customer experiences and optimize product recommendations creates opportunities for increased sales and, consequently, diversified income streams.

7. **Navigating the AI-driven financial landscape:** In the financial sector, AI's application for algorithmic trading, robo-advisors, and risk management presents lucrative avenues. Investors and financial institutions can explore complementary income streams by integrating AI-driven tools into traditional financial services, offering a blend of automation and personalized advice.

8. **Developing AI-enabled educational platforms:** Educational platforms incorporating AI for personalized learning, adaptive assessments, and intelligent tutoring systems are on the rise. Entrepreneurs in the education sector can explore complementary income by combining subscription-based models, licensing AI tools, and offering tailored educational solutions.

9. **Building AI-driven SaaS solutions:** Developing Software as a Service (SaaS) solutions with embedded AI functionalities provides an ongoing revenue stream. Businesses can offer AI-driven tools for data analysis, automation, or customer relationship management, creating a subscription-based income model that ensures regular cash flow.

10. **Implementing AI for cybersecurity solutions:** With the growing concerns around cybersecurity, AI-powered threat detection and response solutions offer valuable income opportunities. Integrating AI into cybersecurity services, including anomaly detection and predictive analysis, allows companies to provide comprehensive protection while establishing a steady revenue stream.

Identifying complementary AI income streams is a strategic imperative for individuals and businesses navigating the AI landscape. By diversifying across industries, services, and business models, stakeholders can build a resilient portfolio that adapts to market dynamics. This essay has explored various strategies, from creating synergies between AI services to leveraging AI in content creation, e-commerce, finance, education, and cybersecurity. The key to sustained success lies in understanding the multifaceted nature of AI applications and strategically positioning oneself to harness complementary income streams effectively.

Thinking Beyond Conventional AI Uses

In this section, we will delve into the realm of unconventional AI use cases, shedding light on innovative and unexpected ways in which AI technologies are making a significant impact. By pushing the boundaries of traditional applications, these use cases challenge preconceived notions and open new avenues for exploration.

1. **AI in wildlife conservation:** Unconventional AI use cases include wildlife conservation efforts. AI-powered drones equipped with computer vision can monitor and protect endangered species. By analyzing animal behavior and tracking poaching activities, AI contributes to safeguarding biodiversity and preserving ecosystems.

2. **AI for mental health support:** Addressing mental health challenges is an emerging area where AI plays a transformative role. Chatbots and virtual assistants powered by natural language processing offer empathetic conversations, providing immediate support and resources to individuals struggling with mental health issues.

3. **AI in art and creativity:** AI's creative capabilities extend to generating art, music, and literature. Generative models like GPT-3 and DeepArt enable the creation of unique artworks, compositions, and even poetry. Collaborations between artists and AI systems redefine the boundaries of human-machine creativity.

4. **AI for agricultural sustainability:** Unconventional AI use cases in agriculture focus on sustainability. AI-driven precision farming optimizes resource allocation, monitors crop health, and predicts disease outbreaks. This innovative approach enhances yields while minimizing environmental impact.

5. **AI in archaeology and historical reconstruction:** Archaeologists leverage AI to analyze historical artifacts and

reconstruct ancient sites. Machine learning algorithms process vast amounts of data, aiding in the interpretation of historical mysteries and contributing to a deeper understanding of our past.

6. **AI-powered journalism and content creation:** AI algorithms contribute to content creation in journalism by automating routine tasks such as fact-checking, data analysis, and even generating news articles. This unconventional use case streamlines journalistic workflows and enhances information dissemination.

7. **AI for space exploration:** Space agencies employ AI in spacecraft navigation, autonomous rovers, and analyzing vast datasets from telescopes. AI's ability to process complex astronomical data accelerates discoveries, aiding humanity's exploration of the cosmos.

8. **AI in human resources for diversity and inclusion:** Unconventional AI use cases in HR involve fostering diversity and inclusion. AI algorithms analyze hiring practices, identify biases, and recommend strategies to create more inclusive workplaces. This application contributes to building diverse and equitable organizations.

9. **AI for wildlife sound recognition:** Acoustic monitoring using AI allows for the identification of wildlife based on sound patterns. This technology aids conservationists in tracking animal populations, studying migration patterns, and assessing the health of ecosystems.

10. **AI in disaster response and humanitarian aid:** AI technologies are utilized in disaster response to analyze satellite imagery, predict natural disasters, and coordinate relief efforts. These unconventional applications enhance the

efficiency and effectiveness of humanitarian aid in crisis situations.

The exploration of unconventional AI use cases demonstrates the versatility and transformative potential of AI technologies. From wildlife conservation and mental health support to art creation and agricultural sustainability, AI continues to redefine the boundaries of what is possible. As researchers, innovators, and industries embrace these unconventional applications, the impact of AI on various aspects of our lives is set to expand, unlocking innovative possibilities and contributing to a more technologically advanced and interconnected world.

Chapter 7:

Optimizing for Long-Term Success

There are certain considerations that are crucial in ensuring that an AI model remains relevant in the ever-changing landscape of exponentially evolving AI. Retention of agility is absolutely crucial, and this can best be achieved by being familiar with which tools are most useful in embedding your AI with properties that optimize its ability to adapt in an ever-shifting market.

Adapting to Market Changes

Remaining Agile in the Face of Disruption

The ability to gather diverse and relevant data is paramount for constructing responsible and agile models. Web scraping, the automated extraction of information from websites, emerges as a powerful tool in this endeavor. This chapter explores the ethical considerations, technical aspects, and benefits of utilizing web scrapers to build AI models that not only perform effectively but also adhere to responsible data practices.

Ethical Considerations in Web Scraping

1. **Respecting terms of service and legal compliance:** Web scraping must be conducted ethically and legally. Respect for the terms of service of websites is crucial, and developers should be aware of legal boundaries to ensure compliance with regulations such as the General Data Protection

Regulation (GDPR) and the Digital Millennium Copyright Act (DMCA).

2. **Prioritizing user privacy:** Ethical web scraping involves prioritizing user privacy. Developers must take measures to anonymize and secure collected data, ensuring that personally identifiable information (PII) is handled responsibly. Implementing techniques like data aggregation and de-identification enhances privacy protection.

3. **Transparency and informed consent:** Transparency is key when utilizing web scraping for data collection, and providing clear information to users about the data collection process, purposes, and potential impacts fosters trust. Informed consent mechanisms should be implemented where applicable.

4. **Avoiding disruption and overloading servers:** Responsible web scraping involves avoiding disruption to the websites being scraped. Developers should implement rate limiting and other techniques to prevent overloading servers, ensuring that the scraping process does not adversely affect the availability of the website for other users.

Technical Aspects of Web Scraping for AI Models

1. **Selecting the right tools:** Choosing suitable web scraping tools is essential. Platforms like BeautifulSoup, Scrapy, and Selenium offer diverse capabilities for extracting data from websites. The selection depends on the complexity of the target sites and the specific requirements of the AI model.

2. **Defining clear objectives:** Before implementing web scraping, clearly define the objectives of data collection. Understanding the data needs of the AI model helps in

crafting effective scraping strategies, ensuring that the gathered information aligns with the intended use and goals of the model.

3. **Handling dynamic content:** Many modern websites use dynamic content loaded through JavaScript. Web scrapers need to handle such dynamic elements. Tools like Selenium enable the automation of browser interactions, facilitating the extraction of data from pages with dynamic content.

4. **Data cleaning and preprocessing:** Raw data obtained through web scraping often requires cleaning and preprocessing. Removing noise, handling missing values, and standardizing formats contribute to the quality of the dataset. This step is crucial for building robust and accurate AI models.

Benefits of Web Scraping in AI Model Development

1. **Enabling diverse data sources:** Web scraping allows access to a wide array of data sources, enriching AI models with diverse information. This diversity enhances the model's ability to generalize and perform well across various scenarios.

2. **Agility in data collection:** Traditional methods of data collection may be time-consuming and inflexible. Web scraping offers agility by quickly adapting to changes in data requirements or incorporating additional sources, facilitating a more responsive AI model development process.

3. **Real-time updates and monitoring:** Continuous monitoring of websites allows for real-time updates and ensures that the AI model remains relevant. Web scrapers can be configured to fetch the latest data, keeping the model up-to-date with changing trends and patterns.

4. **Cost-effective data acquisition:** Web scraping provides a cost-effective means of acquiring data compared to manual methods or purchasing datasets. This affordability empowers developers, researchers, and organizations with limited budgets to access the data they need.

Web scraping stands as a valuable ally in the quest to build responsible and agile AI models. When approached ethically, with considerations for user privacy and legal compliance, web scraping becomes a versatile tool for data acquisition. Its technical aspects, including tool selection, dynamic content handling, and data preprocessing, contribute to the effectiveness of the collected data.

The benefits of web scraping, from enabling diverse data sources to offering agility in data collection, showcase its significance in the AI model development lifecycle. As technology advances, responsible and informed use of web scrapers empowers developers to harness the wealth of information available on the web, contributing to the creation of AI models that not only perform well but also adhere to ethical standards.

Exploring Exit Strategies for AI Entrepreneurs

The easiest way to deploy exit strategies in the AI field is by building and deploying custom AIs that are tailor-made for specific businesses. This can be done through the recently launched AI marketplace by Open AI. Similar to the App Store or Google Play, developers can now create their own custom AI and chatbots and release them through the Open AI App Store for a fee. An alternative to this exit strategy would be to construct your own platform or website to allow users to interact with your AI directly, as is the case in the case study of DoNotPay: an AI product that was designed by a Stanford Computer Science student that helps drivers take on legal cases related to Consumer Protection laws and traffic violations.

Case Study: AI Ventures With Positive Social Impact and the Role of Entrepreneurs in Shaping Ethical Standards

In the realm of consumer protection and legal innovation, DoNotPay stands as a pioneering force, challenging traditional legal practices through the use of AI. Founded by Joshua Browder (Allyn, 2023), a young entrepreneur and computer science whiz, DoNotPay emerged as a tool designed to empower consumers facing legal challenges. This essay delves into the history of DoNotPay, exploring its evolution, the positive impact on consumer protection, and the challenges it poses to the legal profession. Furthermore, it examines the broader implications of AI disruption on white-collar professions and the potential transformation of the legal landscape.

The Genesis of DoNotPay

DoNotPay's inception traces back to 2015, when Browder, then a student at Stanford University, created the platform as a response to the bureaucracy-laden world of consumer law. The initial goal was to simplify the process of contesting parking tickets, a common frustration for many. Through a chatbot interface, users could input their ticket details, and DoNotPay would generate an appeal letter, streamlining an otherwise cumbersome process. This was initially created as a product for personal use. Joshua had accumulated dozens of traffic infractions that he did not have the capacity to pay and realized that if he familiarized himself with the nuances of the law, some, if not all, of these penalties could be dismissed in court. As word began to spread about his success rate, friends and family members began to contact him with their own traffic penalty cases, and before long, he decided to build a website that would streamline the process for anyone contesting their parking violations through the use of AI: effectively creating the world's first "robot lawyer."

Consumer Empowerment

DoNotPay quickly expanded its scope beyond parking tickets. Browder's vision was to democratize legal assistance, making it accessible to everyone. The platform evolved to cover an array of consumer issues, including disputing unfair bank fees, canceling subscriptions effortlessly, and filing small claims lawsuits. The AI-driven chatbot essentially acted as a virtual lawyer, guiding users through legal procedures without the need for expensive legal representation. The AI was so effective that it was presented with a lawsuit for the unlicensed practice of law, a case in which it actually won (Merken, 2023).

Positive Social Impact

DoNotPay has been instrumental in increasing access to justice for individuals who might otherwise be unable to afford legal assistance. This aligns with the broader goal of reducing the justice gap, ensuring that legal remedies are not reserved solely for those with financial means. The platform serves as an educational tool, providing users with insights into their rights and legal options. By demystifying legal processes, DoNotPay empowers individuals to navigate the complexities of the legal system independently. Through its automated processes, DoNotPay has challenged unjust practices, such as the notorious "robosigning" of legal documents by banks. The platform's efficiency in filing mass complaints has contributed to regulatory scrutiny and, in some cases, policy changes.

Challenges to the Legal Profession

1. **Automation and job displacement:** One of the significant challenges posed by DoNotPay is the potential for automation to displace certain legal jobs. Tasks that were traditionally handled by junior lawyers or paralegals, such as

document preparation and simple dispute resolution, can now be automated through AI.

2. **Erosion of billable hours:** Traditional law firms relying on billable hours for revenue may face challenges when users turn to AI-powered platforms like DoNotPay. The efficiency and cost-effectiveness of automated legal assistance can disrupt the traditional billing models, forcing law firms to adapt.

3. **Shift in legal practice:** The rise of platforms like DoNotPay signals a shift in legal practice from routine, repetitive tasks to more complex and strategic work that requires human expertise. Lawyers may need to focus on higher-value services, emphasizing their unique skills in analysis, negotiation, and client counseling.

AI Disruption Across White-Collar Professions

1. **Financial advisory services:** AI-powered algorithms are increasingly used in financial advisory services for tasks like portfolio management, risk assessment, and investment recommendations. This disrupts traditional financial advisory roles, necessitating a shift toward more consultative and strategic financial planning.

2. **Healthcare diagnostics:** In the medical field, AI has demonstrated remarkable capabilities in diagnostics and treatment planning. Radiologists, for instance, may find aspects of their roles being automated, requiring them to adapt to a collaborative model where human expertise complements AI insights.

3. **Business process outsourcing:** White-collar professions involved in routine business processes, such as data entry,

customer support, and administrative tasks, face disruption through AI-driven automation. As AI systems become more sophisticated, the demand for certain administrative roles may decline.

The history of DoNotPay exemplifies the transformative potential of AI in consumer protection and legal assistance. While it contributes to a positive social impact by democratizing access to justice, its disruptive influence on the legal profession cannot be ignored. The challenges faced by traditional legal practices underscore the broader trend of AI-driven disruption across white-collar professions.

As AI continues to evolve, industries must adapt to these technological shifts, redefine roles, and emphasize uniquely human skills. The story of DoNotPay serves as a harbinger of the changing landscape, prompting a reevaluation of how we approach legal services and, more broadly, how white-collar professions adapt to the ongoing revolution in artificial intelligence.

In the closing chapter, we will explore the future projected trends in AI: ever-evolving and ever-adapting. Keep in mind that the world of AI is yet in its infancy, and these projections are ever-changing. The reader is encouraged to keep abreast with these changes and to bear in mind that even these projections could radically change even on a monthly basis as more users begin to recognize the influence and importance of AI in shaping the future of human interactions with technology, thus contributing an important component variable in how these changes affect this new frontier.

Chapter 8:

Looking Ahead: the Future of AI Prosperity

Before we enter the proverbial time machine to get a glimpse into the potential alternative future of AI, it will prove most useful to first assess the blunders that have been made in progressive institutions attempting to utilize AI to optimize otherwise exhaustingly bureaucratic systems. One such case is that of the Dutch government in the Netherlands, which attempted to automate asylum seekers' benefit applications with the use of AI.

Addressing Bias in AI Models

The promise of efficiency and accuracy presented by the use of AI-automated systems often overshadows the potential pitfalls. The recent Dutch scandal serves as a stark reminder that blind reliance on algorithms can have severe consequences, shedding light on the ethical and societal challenges associated with AI implementation (Heikkilä, 2022).

The Dutch Scandal: Unraveling the Algorithmic Blunder

The Dutch scandal revolves around the Dutch Tax and Customs Administration's (Belastingdienst) use of algorithms to detect potential fraud in childcare benefits. The system, designed to identify irregularities and ensure fiscal integrity, ended up disproportionately targeting families with dual nationality, particularly those with a migration background. The heart of the issue lies in algorithmic bias, where the AI system, likely unintentionally, perpetuated discriminatory outcomes. By relying on historical data that already reflected systemic biases, the algorithm amplified and perpetuated the existing inequalities. The consequences were dire, with numerous families unfairly accused of fraud, facing financial ruin and personal distress.

One of the key blunders highlighted by the Dutch scandal is the lack of transparency in the AI decision-making process. The intricate algorithms used by government agencies often operate as black boxes, making it challenging for affected individuals to understand, question, or challenge the outcomes. This opacity diminishes accountability, leaving those affected in a state of vulnerability. The Dutch scandal underscores the ethical considerations surrounding AI deployment. As AI systems become integral to decision-making in various sectors, including healthcare, finance, and law enforcement, it is imperative to address ethical concerns. Ensuring fairness, transparency, and accountability must be at the forefront of AI development to prevent the perpetuation of biases and discriminatory outcomes.

While AI offers unparalleled processing power and data analysis capabilities, the Dutch scandal illuminates the importance of retaining a human-centric approach. Human oversight is crucial to interpreting, questioning, and rectifying the outcomes of AI systems. Striking the right balance between AI assistance and human decision-making is essential to mitigate the risks associated with algorithmic blunders.

Learning from Mistakes: Toward Ethical AI Practices

The Dutch scandal serves as a cautionary tale, urging policymakers, developers, and organizations to reevaluate their approach to AI implementation. It highlights the necessity of thorough testing, ongoing evaluation, and continuous refinement of algorithms to minimize biases and discriminatory effects.

In the wake of the scandal, the imperative for responsible AI practices becomes clearer than ever. Recognizing the potential blunders of AI, actively working to address biases, and increasing transparency are essential steps toward ensuring that AI serves society equitably. As we harness the power of AI, let us do so responsibly, prioritizing ethical considerations to avoid the pitfalls that can arise when algorithms go astray.

Expert Predictions on the Future of AI

AI is propelling us into an era of unprecedented possibilities and transformations. As we gaze into the future, several key trends emerge, shaping the trajectory of AI development. In the next five years, we can anticipate an intensified integration of AI in various sectors. Technologies such as natural language processing (NLP) and computer vision will become more sophisticated, amplifying their applications in business processes, customer interactions, and beyond (Bennett, 2022).

In the coming decade, the evolution of AI promises even more profound changes. Increased AI democratization is foreseen, with accessibility expanding across industries. This is set to radically transform the scientific method that has been in place since the Age of Enlightenment in the 1700s (Tewari, 2022). This means that newer scientific discoveries could be exponentially accelerated by leveraging the break-neck speeds at which AI systems are able to process data through deep learning to extrapolate new theories previously undiscovered by humans. New mathematical theories and the bridging of seemingly unrelated theories could be established, thus allowing theories from one field to be transposed into a completely different field and creating a foundation for an entirely new set of discoveries. In this sense, AI could be used in the same sense as Laplace Transforms in calculus: converting incalculable equations into a new domain where they are solvable and then converting that solution back into the original format in which it could not initially be solved, thus achieving the impossible. This democratization will empower businesses of all sizes to harness AI's capabilities, fostering innovation and competitiveness. Secondly, AI's role in strategic decision-making will become more prominent, aiding leaders in making data-driven choices. Additionally, AI's capacity for personalized experiences will heighten, enhancing customer engagement and satisfaction. The fusion of AI with other cutting-edge technologies, such as the Internet of Things

(IoT) and 5G, is poised to redefine connectivity. Lastly, ethical considerations and responsible AI practices will take center stage, ensuring the development and deployment of AI align with societal values and principles.

This trajectory signifies a future where AI not only augments our capabilities but also becomes an integral part of our daily lives. As we navigate this AI-driven landscape, continuous vigilance and ethical stewardship will be essential to harnessing its benefits while mitigating potential risks. The journey ahead promises a dynamic interplay between human ingenuity and AI innovation, shaping a future that is both exciting and brimming with possibilities.

In Conclusion

We have explored the ethical considerations with regard to the use of AI. On agreeing on the fact that AI use was inevitable, we then proceeded to equip ourselves with all the various most useful and cutting-edge AI tools on the market, along with some introductory instructions on how best to combine and use the tools with some practical examples. After exploring these prefabricated solutions, we delved even deeper into the labyrinth to chart a clear course of the fundamental properties one would need to bear in mind when designing an AI system from scratch using the Python programming language as a point of reference: it is the most widely used program in engineering AI systems. Finally, we looked into a case study of an entrepreneur who built a product from the ground up, namely, the DoNotPay "robot lawyer." We explored some of the backlash they came across, as well as how they are ethically utilizing AI to create a product that benefits consumers by enforcing consumer protection laws. This was done all the better to encourage you on your own journey: do not be intimidated! You will undoubtedly encounter opposition in whatever venture you decide to launch your enterprise in. You'll be disrupting various professions, and particularly when it comes to the disruption of white-collar professions such as law and engineering, the titans that dominate such landscapes are guaranteed to reign down unbridled tyranny on any threats that rise to challenge the monopoly they have enjoyed for centuries. Retaliate with innovation, inspire with tenacity, and perhaps the forthcoming publications on equipping pioneers with revised blueprints for AI entrepreneurs could very well feature your venture!

References

Allyn, B. (2023, January 25). *A robot was scheduled to argue in court, then came the jail threats.* NPR. https://www.npr.org/2023/01/25/1151435033/a-robot-was-scheduled-to-argue-in-court-then-came-the-jail-threats

Bennett, M. (2023, May 25). *The future of AI: What to expect in the next 5 Years.* Enterprise AI. https://www.techtarget.com/searchenterpriseai/tip/The-future-of-AI-What-to-expect-in-the-next-5-years

Eisenmann, T. (2021). *Why startups fail: A new roadmap for entrepreneurial success.* United States: Crown.

Heikkilä, M. (2022, March 29). *Dutch scandal serves as a warning for Europe over risks of using algorithms.* POLITICO. https://www.politico.eu/article/dutch-scandal-serves-as-a-warning-for-europe-over-risks-of-using-algorithms/

Introducing the GPT store. (2024, January 10). Openai.com. https://openai.com/blog/introducing-the-gpt-store

Merken, S. (2023, November 18). *"Robot lawyer" DoNotPay beats lawsuit by Illinois law firm.* Reuters. https://www.reuters.com/legal/legalindustry/robot-lawyer-donotpay-beats-lawsuit-by-illinois-law-firm-2023-11-17/

Says, P. K. M. (2019, March 15). *History of computers: Parts, networking, operating systems, FAQs.* Toppr-Guides. https://www.toppr.com/guides/computer-aptitude-and-knowledge/basics-of-computers/history-of-computers/#:~:text=Early%20History%20of%20Computer&text=One%20of%20the%20earliest%20and

Tewari, G. (2022, May 5). *Council post: The future of AI: 5 Things to expect in the next 10 years.* Forbes. https://www.forbes.com/sites/forbesbusinesscouncil/2022/05/05/the-future-of-ai-5-things-to-expect-in-the-next-10-years/?sh=1293418f7422

Watson, I. (2012, April 26). *How Alan Turing invented the computer age.* Scientific American Blog Network. https://blogs.scientificamerican.com/guest-blog/how-alan-turing-invented-the-computer-age/